FRENCH GRAMMAR

Collins Gem

An imprint of HarperCollins*Publishers*

first published in this edition 1994

© HarperCollins Publishers 1994

latest reprint 1999

ISBN 0 00 470999-3 Paperback

Lesley A Robertson MA
Lorna Sinclair-Knight BA, PhD

editorial staff
Christine Penman, Megan Thomson

editorial management
Vivian Marr

A catalogue record for this book is
available from the British Library

Typeset by Tradespools Ltd, Frome, Somerset

Printed and bound in Great Britain by
Caledonian International Book Manufacturing Ltd,
Glasgow, G64

INTRODUCTION

The **Collins Gem French Grammar** is designed to offer students of French of all ages and at all levels an uncluttered, step-by-step guide to the grammar of the language. For the person with little or no knowledge of French it provides the basic 'tools' necessary for comprehension and communication, and for the more advanced learner it provides an efficient and speedy means of reference and revision.

As you will see from the contents list overleaf, the book is split into sections according to part of speech (nouns, articles, adjectives etc) or grammar point (sentence structure, use of numbers etc). As far as is possible, we have tried to anticipate any grammatical terms with which you may not be familiar, and a brief explanation is given at the relevant point in the text.

A special feature of this book is the clear demarcation of grammatical points, each of which is treated on a left-hand page and illustrated by numerous practical, up-to-date examples on the opposite right-hand page. For instance, turn to page 154 and you will see a series of bracketed numbers (→1) to (→10) throughout the text on that page. These numbers cross-refer you to an example, or group of examples, on page 155. This double-page layout gives you maximum accessibility to the grammar point you want to learn or revise, while the examples help fix that grammar point firmly in your mind.

Special attention is paid throughout the book to potential problem areas – such as sentence structure, where French usage can differ markedly from English usage. In addition, the section on translation problems alerts you to some of the most common pitfalls of translation. A full index, with both grammatical topics and key words in French and English, completes the grammar.

ABBREVIATIONS USED

ctd.	continued	**p(p).**	page(s)	**qn**	quelqu'un
fem.	feminine	**perf.**	perfect	**sb**	somebody
infin.	infinitive	**plur.**	plural	**sing.**	singular
masc.	masculine	**qch**	quelque chose	**sth**	something

4 CONTENTS

VERBS

NOUNS

ARTICLES

ADJECTIVES

Simple Tenses: formation

In French the simple tenses are:

Present	(→ **1**)
Imperfect	(→ **2**)
Future	(→ **3**)
Conditional	(→ **4**)
Past Historic	(→ **5**)
Present Subjunctive	(→ **6**)
Imperfect Subjunctive	(→ **7**)

They are formed by adding endings to a verb stem. The endings show the number and person of the subject of the verb (→ **8**)

The stem and endings of regular verbs are totally predictable. The following sections show all the patterns for regular verbs. For irregular verbs see pp. 74 ff.

Regular Verbs

There are three regular verb patterns (called conjugations), each identifiable by the ending of the infinitive:

● First conjugation verbs end in **-er** e.g. **donner** to give

● Second conjugation verbs end in **-ir** e.g. **finir** to finish

● Third conjugation verbs end in **-re** e.g. **vendre** to sell

These three conjugations are treated in order on the following pages.

Continued

1 je donne
I give, I am giving, I do give

2 je donnais
I gave, I was giving, I used to give

3 je donnerai
I shall give, I shall be giving

4 je donnerais
I should/would give, I should/would be giving

5 je donnai
I gave

6 (que) je donne
(that) I give/gave

7 (que) je donnasse
(that) I gave

8 je donne   I give
nous donnons   we give
je donnerais   I would give
nous donnerions   we would give

Simple Tenses: First Conjugation

● The stem is formed as follows:

TENSE	FORMATION	EXAMPLE
Present		
Imperfect		
Past Historic	} infinitive minus -er	donn-
Present Subjunctive		
Imperfect Subjunctive		
Future	} infinitive	donner-
Conditional		

● To the appropriate stem add the following endings:

		PRESENT (→1)	IMPERFECT (→2)	PAST HISTORIC (→3)
sing.	1st person	-e	-ais	-ai
	2nd person	-es	-ais	-as
	3rd person	-e	-ait	-a
plur.	1st person	-ons	-ions	-âmes
	2nd person	-ez	-iez	-âtes
	3rd person	-ent	-aient	-èrent

		PRESENT SUBJUNCTIVE (→4)	IMPERFECT SUBJUNCTIVE (→5)
sing.	1st person	-e	-asse
	2nd person	-es	-asses
	3rd person	-e	-ât
plur.	1st person	-ions	-assions
	2nd person	-iez	-assiez
	3rd person	-ent	-assent

		FUTURE (→6)	CONDITIONAL (→7)
sing.	1st person	-ai	-ais
	2nd person	-as	-ais
	3rd person	-a	-ait
plur.	1st person	-ons	-ions
	2nd person	-ez	-iez
	3rd person	-ont	-aient

	1 PRESENT		**2** IMPERFECT		**3** PAST HISTORIC
je	donne	je	donnais	je	donnai
tu	donnes	tu	donnais	tu	donnas
il	donne	il	donnait	il	donna
elle	donne	elle	donnait	elle	donna
nous	donnons	nous	donnions	nous	donnâmes
vous	donnez	vous	donniez	vous	donnâtes
ils	donnent	ils	donnaient	ils	donnèrent
elles	donnent	elles	donnaient	elles	donnèrent

	4 PRESENT SUBJUNCTIVE		**5** IMPERFECT SUBJUNCTIVE
je	donne	je	donnasse
tu	donnes	tu	donnasses
il	donne	il	donnât
elle	donne	elle	donnât
nous	donnions	nous	donnassions
vous	donniez	vous	donnassiez
ils	donnent	ils	donnassent
elles	donnent	elles	donnassent

	6 FUTURE		**7** CONDITIONAL
je	donnerai	je	donnerais
tu	donneras	tu	donnerais
il	donnera	il	donnerait
elle	donnera	elle	donnerait
nous	donnerons	nous	donnerions
vous	donnerez	vous	donneriez
ils	donneront	ils	donneraient
elles	donneront	elles	donneraient

Simple Tenses: Second Conjugation

● The stem is formed as follows:

TENSE	FORMATION	EXAMPLE
Present		
Imperfect		
Past Historic	infinitive minus -ir	**fin-**
Present Subjunctive		
Imperfect Subjunctive		
Future	infinitive	**finir-**
Conditional		

● To the appropriate stem add the following endings:

		PRESENT (→1)	IMPERFECT (→2)	PAST HISTORIC (→3)
sing.	1st person	-is	-issais	-is
	2nd person	-is	-issais	-is
	3rd person	-it	-issait	-it
plur.	1st person	-issons	-issions	-îmes
	2nd person	-issez	-issiez	-îtes
	3rd person	-issent	-issaient	-irent

		PRESENT SUBJUNCTIVE (→4)	IMPERFECT SUBJUNCTIVE (→5)
sing.	1st person	-isse	-isse
	2nd person	-isses	-isses
	3rd person	-isse	-ît
plur.	1st person	-issions	-issions
	2nd person	-issiez	-issiez
	3rd person	-issent	-issent

		FUTURE (→6)	CONDITIONAL (→7)
sing.	1st person	-ai	-ais
	2nd person	-as	-ais
	3rd person	-a	-ait
plur.	1st person	-ons	-ions
	2nd person	-ez	-iez
	3rd person	-ont	-aient

1 *PRESENT*

je	finis
tu	finis
il	finit
elle	finit
nous	finissons
vous	finissez
ils	finissent
elles	finissent

2 *IMPERFECT*

je	finissais
tu	finissais
il	finissait
elle	finissait
nous	finissions
vous	finissiez
ils	finissaient
elles	finissaient

3 *PAST HISTORIC*

je	finis
tu	finis
il	finit
elle	finit
nous	finîmes
vous	finîtes
ils	finirent
elles	finirent

4 *PRESENT SUBJUNCTIVE*

je	finisse
tu	finisses
il	finisse
elle	finisse
nous	finissions
vous	finissiez
ils	finissent
elles	finissent

5 *IMPERFECT SUBJUNCTIVE*

je	finisse
tu	finisses
il	finît
elle	finît
nous	finissions
vous	finissiez
ils	finissent
elles	finissent

6 *FUTURE*

je	finirai
tu	finiras
il	finira
elle	finira
nous	finirons
vous	finirez
ils	finiront
elles	finiront

7 *CONDITIONAL*

je	finirais
tu	finirais
il	finirait
elle	finirait
nous	finirions
vous	finiriez
ils	finiraient
elles	finiraient

Simple Tenses: Third Conjugation

● The stem is formed as follows:

TENSE	FORMATION	EXAMPLE
Present		
Imperfect		
Past Historic	infinitive minus **-re**	**vend-**
Present Subjunctive		
Imperfect Subjunctive		
Future	infinitive minus **-e**	**vendr-**
Conditional		

● To the appropriate stem add the following endings:

		PRESENT (→1)	IMPERFECT (→2)	PAST HISTORIC (→3)
sing.	1st person	-s	-ais	-is
	2nd person	-s	-ais	-is
	3rd person	–	-ait	-it
plur.	1st person	-ons	-ions	-îmes
	2nd person	-ez	-iez	-îtes
	3rd person	-ent	-aient	-irent

		PRESENT SUBJUNCTIVE (→4)	IMPERFECT SUBJUNCTIVE (→5)
sing.	1st person	-e	-isse
	2nd person	-es	-isses
	3rd person	-e	-ît
plur.	1st person	-ions	-issions
	2nd person	-iez	-issiez
	3rd person	-ent	-issent

		FUTURE (→6)	CONDITIONAL (→7)
sing.	1st person	-ai	-ais
	2nd person	-as	-ais
	3rd person	-a	-ait
plur.	1st person	-ons	-ions
	2nd person	-ez	-iez
	3rd person	-ont	-aient

1 *PRESENT*		**2** *IMPERFECT*		**3** *PAST HISTORIC*	
je	vend**s**	je	vend**ais**	je	vend**is**
tu	vend**s**	tu	vend**ais**	tu	vend**is**
il	vend	il	vend**ait**	il	vend**it**
elle	vend	elle	vend**ait**	elle	vend**it**
nous	vend**ons**	nous	vend**ions**	nous	vend**îmes**
vous	vend**ez**	vous	vend**iez**	vous	vend**îtes**
ils	vend**ent**	ils	vend**aient**	ils	vend**irent**
elles	vend**ent**	elles	vend**aient**	elles	vend**irent**

4 *PRESENT SUBJUNCTIVE*		**5** *IMPERFECT SUBJUNCTIVE*	
je	vend**e**	je	vend**isse**
tu	vend**es**	tu	vend**isses**
il	vend**e**	il	vend**ît**
elle	vend**e**	elle	vend**ît**
nous	vend**ions**	nous	vend**issions**
vous	vend**iez**	vous	vend**issiez**
ils	vend**ent**	ils	vend**issent**
elles	vend**ent**	elles	vend**issent**

6 *FUTURE*		**7** *CONDITIONAL*	
je	vend**rai**	je	vend**rais**
tu	vend**ras**	tu	vend**rais**
il	vend**ra**	il	vend**rait**
elle	vend**ra**	elle	vend**rait**
nous	vend**rons**	nous	vend**rions**
vous	vend**rez**	vous	vend**riez**
ils	vend**ront**	ils	vend**raient**
elles	vend**ront**	elles	vend**raient**

First Conjugation Spelling Irregularities

Before certain endings, the stems of some '-er' verbs may change slightly.

Below, and on subsequent pages, the verb types are identified, and the changes described are illustrated by means of a representative verb.

Verbs ending:	**-cer**
Change:	**c** becomes **ç** before **a** or **o**
Tenses affected:	Present, Imperfect, Past Historic, Imperfect Subjunctive, Present Participle
Model:	**lancer** to throw (→ **1**)

● Why the change occurs:
   A cedilla is added to the **c** to retain its soft [s] pronunciation before the vowels **a** and **o**

Verbs ending:	**-ger**
Change:	**g** becomes **ge** before **a** or **o**
Tenses affected:	Present, Imperfect, Past Historic, Imperfect Subjunctive, Present Participle
Model:	**manger** to eat (→ **2**)

● Why the change occurs:
   An **e** is added after the **g** to retain its soft [ʒ] pronunciation before the vowels **a** and **o**

Continued

1

INFINITIVE	PRESENT PARTICIPLE
lancer	**lançant**

PRESENT		IMPERFECT	
je	lance	**je**	**lançais**
tu	lances	**tu**	**lançais**
il/elle	lance	**il/elle**	**lançait**
nous	**lançons**	nous	lancions
vous	lancez	vous	lanciez
ils/elles	lancent	**ils/elles**	**lançaient**

PAST HISTORIC		IMPERFECT SUBJUNCTIVE	
je	**lançai**	je	lançasse
tu	**lanças**	tu	lançasses
il/elle	**lança**	il/elle	lançât
nous	**lançâmes**	nous	lançassions
vous	**lançâtes**	vous	lançassiez
ils/elles	lancèrent	**ils/elles**	**lançassent**

2

INFINITIVE	PRESENT PARTICIPLE
manger	**mangeant**

PRESENT		IMPERFECT	
je	mange	**je**	**mangeais**
tu	manges	**tu**	**mangeais**
il/elle	mange	**il/elle**	**mangeait**
nous	**mangeons**	nous	mangions
vous	mangez	vous	mangiez
ils/elles	mangent	**ils/elles**	**mangeaient**

PAST HISTORIC		IMPERFECT SUBJUNCTIVE	
je	**mangeai**	**je**	**mangeasse**
tu	**mangeas**	**tu**	**mangeasses**
il/elle	**mangea**	il/elle	mangeât
nous	**mangeâmes**	**nous**	**mangeassions**
vous	**mangeâtes**	**vous**	**mangeassiez**
ils/elles	mangèrent	**ils/elles**	**mangeassent**

First Conjugation Spelling Irregularities (ctd.)

Verbs ending   **-eler**
Change: **-l** doubles before **-e**, **-es**, **-ent** and throughout the
     Future and Conditional tenses
Tenses affected: Present, Present Subjunctive, Future, Conditional
Model: **appeler** to call (→ 1)

- Exceptions: **geler** to freeze } like **mener** (p. 18)
               peler to peel

Verbs ending   **-eter**
Change: **-t** doubles before **-e**, **es**, **-ent** and throughout the
     Future and Conditional tenses
Tenses affected: Present, Present Subjunctive, Future, Conditional
Model: **jeter** to throw (→ 2)

- Exceptions: **acheter** to buy } like **mener** (p. 18)
               haleter to pant

Verbs ending   **-yer**
Change: **y** changes to **i** before **-e**, **-es**, **-ent** and throughout
     the Future and Conditional tenses
Tenses affected: Present, Present Subjunctive, Future, Conditional
Model: **essuyer** to wipe (→ 3)

- The change described is optional for verbs ending in **-ayer** e.g.
payer to pay, **essayer** to try

Continued

1 *PRESENT (+ SUBJUNCTIVE)*   *FUTURE*

j'appelle   j'appellerai
tu appelles   tu appelleras
il/elle appelle   il appellera *etc.*
nous appelons
(appelions)   *CONDITIONAL*

vous appelez   j'appellerais
(appeliez)   tu appellerais
ils/elles appellent   il appellerait *etc.*

2 *PRESENT (+ SUBJUNCTIVE)*   *FUTURE*

je jette   je jetterai
tu jettes   tu jetteras
il/elle jette   il jettera *etc.*
nous jetons
(jetions)   *CONDITIONAL*

vous jetez   je jetterais
(jetiez)   tu jetterais
ils/elles jettent   il jetterait *etc.*

3 *PRESENT (+ SUBJUNCTIVE)*   *FUTURE*

j'essuie   j'essuierai
tu essuies   tu essuieras
il/elle essuie   il essuiera *etc.*
nous essuyons
(essuyions)   *CONDITIONAL*

vous essuyez   j'essuierais
(essuyiez)   tu essuierais
ils/elles essuient   il essuierait *etc.*

First Conjugation Spelling Irregularities (ctd.)

Verbs ending	**mener, peser, lever** etc
Change:	**e** changes to **è**, before -e, -es, -ent and throughout the Future and Conditional tenses
Tenses affected:	Present, Present Subjunctive, Future, Conditional
Model:	**mener** to lead (→ **1**)

Verbs like:	**céder, régler, espérer** etc
Change:	**é** changes to **è** before -e, -es, -ent
Tenses affected:	Present, Present Subjunctive
Model:	**céder** to yield (→ **2**)

1 *PRESENT (+ SUBJUNCTIVE)*
        je mène
        tu mènes
   il/elle mène
    nous menons
       (menions)
    vous menez
       (meniez)
 ils/elles mènent

FUTURE
   je mènerai
   tu mèneras
   il mènera *etc.*

CONDITIONAL
   je mènerais
   tu mènerais
   il mènerait *etc.*

2 *PRESENT (+ SUBJUNCTIVE)*
       je cède
       tu cèdes
   il/elle cède
    nous cédons
       (cédions)
    vous cédez
       (cédiez)
 ils/elles cèdent

The Imperative

The imperative is the form of the verb used to give commands or orders. It can be used politely, as in English 'Shut the door, please'.

The imperative is the same as the present tense **tu**, **nous** and **vous** forms without the subject pronouns:

donne*	**finis**	**vends**
give	*finish*	*sell*

*The final 's' of the present tense of first conjugation verbs is dropped, except before **y** and **en** (→ **1**)

donnons	**finissons**	**vendons**
let's give	*let's finish*	*let's sell*

donnez	**finissez**	**vendez**
give	*finish*	*sell*

● The imperative of irregular verbs is given in the verb tables, pp. 74 ff.

● Position of object pronouns with the imperative:
  in POSITIVE commands: they follow the verb and are attached to it by hyphens (→ **2**)
  in NEGATIVE commands: they precede the verb and are not attached to it (→ **3**)

● For the order of object pronouns, see p. 170

● For reflexive verbs – e.g. **se lever** *to get up* – the object pronoun is the reflexive pronoun (→ **4**)

1 Compare: **Tu donnes de l'argent à Paul**
You give (some) money to Paul
and: **Donne de l'argent à Paul**
Give (some) money to Paul

2 **Excusez-moi**   **Envoyons-les-leur**
Excuse me   Let's send them to them
Crois-nous   **Expliquez-le-moi**
Believe us   Explain it to me
Attendons-la   **Rends-la-lui**
Let's wait for her/it   Give it back to him/her

3 **Ne me dérange pas**   **Ne leur en parlons pas**
Don't disturb me   Let's not speak to them about it
Ne les négligeons pas   **N'y pense plus**
Let's not neglect them   Don't think about it any more
Ne leur répondez pas   **Ne la lui rends pas**
Don't answer them   Don't give it back to him/her

4 **Lève-toi**   **Ne te lève pas**
Get up   Don't get up
Dépêchons-nous   **Ne nous affolons pas**
Let's hurry   Let's not panic
Levez-vous   **Ne vous levez pas**
Get up   Don't get up

Compound Tenses: formation

In French the compound tenses are:

Perfect	(→ 1)
Pluperfect	(→ 2)
Future Perfect	(→ 3)
Conditional Perfect	(→ 4)
Past Anterior	(→ 5)
Perfect Subjunctive	(→ 6)
Pluperfect Subjunctive	(→ 7)

They consist of the past participle of the verb together with an auxiliary verb. Most verbs take the auxiliary **avoir**, but some take **être** (see p. 28).

Compound tenses are formed in exactly the same way for both regular and irregular verbs, the only difference being that irregular verbs may have an irregular past participle.

The Past Participle

For all compound tenses you need to know how to form the past participle of the verb. For regular verbs this is as follows:

● 1st conjugation: replace the **-er** of the infinitive by **-é** (→ 8)
● 2nd conjugation: replace the **-ir** of the infinitive by **-i** (→ 9)
● 3rd conjugation: replace the **-re** of the infinitive by **-u** (→ 10)

● See p. 50 for agreement of past participles.

Continued

with **avoir**	with **être**
1 j'ai donné I gave, have given	**je suis tombé** I fell, have fallen
2 j'avais donné I had given	**j'étais tombé** I had fallen
3 j'aurai donné I shall have given	**je serai tombé** I shall have fallen
4 j'aurais donné I should/would have given	**je serais tombé** I should/would have fallen
5 j'eus donné I had given	**je fus tombé** I had fallen
6 (que) j'aie donné (that) I gave, have given	**(que) je sois tombé** (that) I fell, have fallen
7 (que) j'eusse donné (that) I had given	**(que) je fusse tombé** (that) I had fallen

8 donner → donné
   to give   given

9 finir → fini
   to finish   finished

10 vendre → vendu
    to sell   sold

Compound Tenses: formation (ctd.)

Verbs taking the auxiliary avoir

Perfect tense:
the present tense of **avoir** plus the past participle (→ **1**)

Pluperfect tense:
the imperfect tense of **avoir** plus the past participle (→ **2**)

Future Perfect:
the future tense of **avoir** plus the past participle (→ **3**)

Conditional Perfect:
the conditional of **avoir** plus the past participle (→ **4**)

Past Anterior:
the past historic of **avoir** plus the past participle (→ **5**)

Perfect Subjunctive:
the present subjunctive of **avoir** plus the past participle (→ **6**)

Pluperfect Subjunctive:
the imperfect subjunctive of **avoir** plus the past participle (→ **7**)

● For how to form the past participle of regular verbs see p. 22. The past participle of irregular verbs is given for each verb in the verb tables, pp. 74 ff.

● The past participle must agree in number and in gender with any preceding direct object (see p. 50)

Continued

1 *PERFECT*
j'ai donné	nous avons donné
tu as donné	vous avez donné
il/elle a donné	ils/elles ont donné

2 *PLUPERFECT*
j'avais donné	nous avions donné
tu avais donné	vous aviez donné
il/elle avait donné	ils/elles avaient donné

3 *FUTURE PERFECT*
j'aurai donné	nous aurons donné
tu auras donné	vous aurez donné
il/elle aura donné	ils/elles auront donné

4 *CONDITIONAL PERFECT*
j'aurais donné	nous aurions donné
tu aurais donné	vous auriez donné
il/elle aurait donné	ils/elles auraient donné

5 *PAST ANTERIOR*
j'eus donné	nous eûmes donné
tu eus donné	vous eûtes donné
il/elle eut donné	ils/elles eurent donné

6 *PERFECT SUBJUNCTIVE*
j'aie donné	nous ayons donné
tu aies donné	vous ayez donné
il/elle ait donné	ils/elles aient donné

7 *PLUPERFECT SUBJUNCTIVE*
j'eusse donné	nous eussions donné
tu eusses donné	vous eussiez donné
il/elle eût donné	ils/elles eussent donné

Compound Tenses: formation (ctd.)

Verbs taking the auxiliary être

Perfect tense: the present tense of **être** plus the past
                            participle (→ **1**)

Pluperfect tense: the imperfect tense of **être** plus the past
                            participle (→ **2**)

Future Perfect: the future tense of **être** plus the past
                            participle (→ **3**)

Conditional Perfect: the conditional of **être** plus the past
                            participle (→ **4**)

Past Anterior: the past historic of **être** plus the past
                            participle (→ **5**)

Perfect Subjunctive: the present subjunctive of **être** plus the past
                            participle (→ **6**)

Pluperfect Subjunctive: the imperfect subjunctive of **être** plus the
                            past participle (→ **7**)

● For how to form the past participle of regular verbs see p. 22. The
  past participle of irregular verbs is given for each verb in the verb
  tables, pp. 74 ff.

● For agreement of past participles, see p. 50

● For a list of verbs and verb types that take the auxiliary **être**, see
  p. 28

Continued

1 *PERFECT*
je suis tombé(e)   nous sommes tombé(e)s
tu es tombé(e)   vous êtes tombé(e)(s)
il est tombé   ils sont tombés
elle est tombée   elles sont tombées

2 *PLUPERFECT*
j'étais tombé(e)   nous étions tombé(e)s
tu étais tombé(e)   vous étiez tombé(e)(s)
il était tombé   ils étaient tombés
elle était tombée   elles étaient tombées

3 *FUTURE PERFECT*
je serai tombé(e)   nous serons tombé(e)s
tu seras tombé(e)   vous serez tombé(e)(s)
il sera tombé   ils seront tombés
elle sera tombée   elles seront tombées

4 *CONDITIONAL PERFECT*
je serais tombé(e)   nous serions tombé(e)s
tu serais tombé(e)   vous seriez tombé(e)(s)
il serait tombé   ils seraient tombés
elle serait tombée   elles seraient tombées

5 *PAST ANTERIOR*
je fus tombé(e)   nous fûmes tombé(e)s
tu fus tombé(e)   vous fûtes tombé(e)(s)
il fut tombé   ils furent tombés
elle fut tombée   elles furent tombées

6 *PERFECT SUBJUNCTIVE*
je sois tombé(e)   nous soyons tombé(e)s
tu sois tombé(e)   vous soyez tombé(e)(s)
il soit tombé   ils soient tombés
elle soit tombée   elles soient tombées

7 *PLUPERFECT SUBJUNCTIVE*
je fusse tombé(e)   nous fussions tombé(e)s
tu fusses tombé(e)   vous fussiez tombé(e)(s)
il fût tombé   ils fussent tombés
elle fût tombée   elles fussent tombées

Compound Tenses (ctd.)

The following verbs take the auxiliary être

● Reflexive verbs (see p. 30) (→ **1**)

● The following intransitive verbs (i.e. verbs which cannot take a direct object), largely expressing motion or a change of state:

aller	to go (→ **2**)	**passer**	to pass
arriver	to arrive; to happen	**rentrer**	to go back/in
descendre	to go/come down	**rester**	to stay (→ **5**)
devenir	to become	**retourner**	to go back
entrer	to go/come in	**revenir**	to come back
monter	to go/come up	**sortir**	to go/come out
mourir	to die (→ **3**)	**tomber**	to fall
naître	to be born	**venir**	to come (→ **6**)
partir	to leave (→ **4**)		

● Of these, the following are conjugated with **avoir** when used transitively (i.e. with a direct object):

descendre	to bring/take down
entrer	to bring/take in
monter	to bring/take up (→ **7**)
passer	to pass; to spend (→ **8**)
rentrer	to bring/take in
retourner	to turn over
sortir	to bring/take out (→ **9**)

● Note that the past participle must show an agreement in number and gender whenever the auxiliary is **être** EXCEPT FOR REFLEXIVE VERBS WHERE THE REFLEXIVE PRONOUN IS THE INDIRECT OBJECT (see p. 50)

1 je me suis arrêté(e)
I stopped
tu t'es levé(e)
you got up

elle s'est trompée
she made a mistake
ils s'étaient battus
they had fought (one another)

2 elle est allée
she went

3 ils sont morts
they died

4 vous êtes partie
you left (*addressing a female person*)
vous êtes parties
you left (*addressing more than one female person*)

5 nous sommes resté(e)s
we stayed

6 elles étaient venues
they [female] had come

7 Il a monté les valises
He's taken up the cases

8 Nous avons passé trois semaines chez elle
We spent three weeks at her place

9 Avez-vous sorti la voiture?
Have you taken the car out?

Reflexive Verbs

A reflexive verb is one accompanied by a reflexive pronoun, e.g. **se
lever** *to get up*; **se laver** *to wash (oneself)*. The pronouns are:

PERSON	SINGULAR	PLURAL
1st	**me (m')**	**nous**
2nd	**te (t')**	**vous**
3rd	**se (s')**	**se (s')**

The forms shown in brackets are used before a vowel, an **h**
'mute', or the pronoun **y** (→ **1**)

● In positive commands, **te** changes to **toi** (→ **2**)

● The reflexive pronoun 'reflects back' to the subject, but it is not
always translated in English (→ **3**)
The plural pronouns are sometimes translated as *one another*, *each
other* (the 'reciprocal' meaning) (→ **4**)
The reciprocal meaning may be emphasised by **l'un(e) l'autre (les
un(e)s les autres)** (→ **5**)

● Simple tenses of reflexive verbs are conjugated in exactly the same
way as those of non-reflexive verbs except that the reflexive
pronoun is always used. Compound tenses are formed with the
auxiliary **être**. A sample reflexive verb is conjugated in full on pp. 34
and 35.

For agreement of past participles, see p. 32

Position of Reflexive Pronouns

● In constructions other than the imperative affirmative the pronoun
comes before the verb (→ **6**)

● In the imperative affirmative, the pronoun follows the verb and is
attached to it by a hyphen (→ **7**)

Continued

1 Je m'ennuie
I'm bored
Elle s'habille
She's getting dressed
Ils s'y intéressent
They are interested in it

2 Assieds-toi
Sit down
Tais-toi
Be quiet

3 Je me prépare
I'm getting (myself) ready
Nous nous lavons
We're washing (ourselves)
Elle se lève
She gets up

4 Nous nous parlons
We speak to each other
Ils se ressemblent
They resemble one another

5 Ils se regardent l'un l'autre
They are looking at each other

6 Je me couche tôt
I go to bed early
Comment vous appelez-vous?
What is your name?
Il ne s'est pas rasé
He hasn't shaved
Ne te dérange pas pour nous
Don't put yourself out on our account

7 Dépêche-toi
Hurry (up)
Renseignons-nous
Let's find out
Asseyez-vous
Sit down

Reflexive Verbs (ctd.)

Past Participle Agreement

- In most reflexive verbs the reflexive pronoun is a DIRECT object pronoun (→ 1)

- When a direct object accompanies the reflexive verb the pronoun is then the INDIRECT object (→ 2)

- The past participle of a reflexive verb agrees in number and gender with a direct object which *precedes* the verb (usually, but not always, the reflexive pronoun) (→ 3)
  The past participle does not change if the direct object follows the verb (→ 4)

Here are some common reflexive verbs:

s'en aller	to go away	se hâter	to hurry
s'amuser	to enjoy oneself	se laver	to wash (oneself)
s'appeler	to be called	se lever	to get up
s'arrêter	to stop	se passer	to happen
s'asseoir	to sit (down)	se promener	to go for a walk
se baigner	to go swimming	se rappeler	to remember
se blesser	to hurt oneself	se ressembler	to resemble each other
se coucher	to go to bed	se retourner	to turn round
se demander	to wonder	se réveiller	to wake up
se dépêcher	to hurry	se sauver	to run away
se diriger	to make one's way	se souvenir de	to remember
s'endormir	to fall asleep	se taire	to be quiet
s'ennuyer	to be/get bored	se tromper	to be mistaken
se fâcher	to get angry	se trouver	to be (situated)
s'habiller	to dress (oneself)		

Continued

Examples

1 Je m'appelle
I'm called (*literally: I call myself*)
Asseyez-vous
Sit down (*literally: Seat yourself*)
Ils se lavent
They wash (themselves)

2 Elle se lave les mains
She's washing her hands (*literally: She's washing to herself the hands*)
Je me brosse les dents
I brush my teeth
Nous nous envoyons des cadeaux à Noël
We send presents to each other at Christmas

3 'Je me suis endormi' s'est-il excusé
'I fell asleep', he apologized
Pauline s'est dirigée vers la sortie
Pauline made her way towards the exit
Ils se sont levés vers dix heures
They got up around ten o'clock
Elles se sont excusées de leur erreur
They apologised for their mistake
Est-ce que tu t'es blessée, Cécile?
Have you hurt yourself, Cécile?

4 Elle s'est lavé les cheveux
She (has) washed her hair
Nous nous sommes serré la main
We shook hands
Christine s'est cassé la jambe
Christine has broken her leg

Reflexive Verbs (ctd.)

Conjugation of: **se laver** to wash (oneself)

I   *SIMPLE TENSES*

PRESENT

je me lave	nous nous lavons
tu te laves	vous vous lavez
il/elle se lave	ils/elles se lavent

IMPERFECT

je me lavais	nous nous lavions
tu te lavais	vous vous laviez
il/elle se lavait	ils/elles se lavaient

FUTURE

je me laverai	nous nous laverons
tu te laveras	vous vous laverez
il/elle se lavera	ils/elles se laveront

CONDITIONAL

je me laverais	nous nous laverions
tu te laverais	vous vous laveriez
il/elle se laverait	ils/elles se laveraient

PAST HISTORIC

je me lavai	nous nous lavâmes
tu te lavas	vous vous lavâtes
il/elle se lava	ils/elles se lavèrent

PRESENT SUBJUNCTIVE

je me lave	nous nous lavions
tu te laves	vous vous laviez
il/elle se lave	ils/elles se lavent

IMPERFECT SUBJUNCTIVE

je me lavasse	nous nous lavassions
tu te lavasses	vous vous lavassiez
il/elle se lavât	ils/elles se lavassent

Reflexive Verbs (ctd.)

Conjugation of: **se laver** *to wash (oneself)*

II *COMPOUND TENSES*

PERFECT

je me suis lavé(e)	nous nous sommes lavé(e)s
tu t'es lavé(e)	vous vous êtes lavé(e)(s)
il/elle s'est lavé(e)	ils/elles se sont lavé(e)s

PLUPERFECT

je m'étais lavé(e)	nous nous étions lavé(e)s
tu t'étais lavé(e)	vous vous étiez lavé(e)(s)
il/elle s'était lavé(e)	ils/elles s'étaient lavé(e)s

FUTURE PERFECT

je me serai lavé(e)	nous nous serons lavé(e)s
tu te seras lavé(e)	vous vous serez lavé(e)(s)
il/elle se sera lavé(e)	ils/elles se seront lavé(e)s

CONDITIONAL PERFECT

je me serais lavé(e)	nous nous serions lavé(e)s
tu te serais lavé(e)	vous vous seriez lavé(e)(s)
il/elle se serait lavé(e)	ils/elles se seraient lavé(e)s

PAST ANTERIOR

je me fus lavé(e)	nous nous fûmes lavé(e)s
tu te fus lavé(e)	vous vous fûtes lavé(e)(s)
il/elle se fut lavé(e)	ils/elles se furent lavé(e)s

PERFECT SUBJUNCTIVE

je me sois lavé(e)	nous nous soyons lavé(e)s
tu te sois lavé(e)	vous vous soyez lavé(e)(s)
il/elle se soit lavé(e)	ils/elles se soient lavé(e)s

PLUPERFECT SUBJUNCTIVE

je me fusse lavé(e)	nous nous fussions lavé(e)s
tu te fusses lavé(e)	vous vous fussiez lavé(e)(s)
il/elle se fût lavé(e)	ils/elles se fussent lavé(e)s

36 VERBS

The Passive

In the passive, the subject *receives* the action (e.g. *I was hit*) as opposed to *performing* it (e.g. *I hit him*). In English the verb 'to be' is used with the past participle. In French the passive is formed in exactly the same way, i.e.:

a tense of **être** + past participle

The past participle agrees in number and gender with the subject (→**1**)

A sample verb is conjugated in the passive voice on pp. 38 and 39.

● The indirect object in French cannot become the subject in the passive:

in **quelqu'un m'a donné un livre** the indirect object **m'** cannot become the subject of a passive verb (unlike English: *someone gave me a book→I was given a book*)

● The passive meaning is often expressed in French by:
   – **on** plus a verb in the active voice (→**2**)
   – a reflexive verb (see p. 30) (→**3**)

Continued

1 Philippe a été récompensé
Phillip has been rewarded
Cette peinture est très admirée
This painting is greatly admired
Ils le feront pourvu qu'ils soient payés
They'll do it provided they're paid
Les enfants seront félicités
The children will be congratulated
Cette mesure aurait été critiquée si ...
This measure would have been criticized if ...
Les portes avaient été fermées
The doors had been closed

2 On leur a envoyé une lettre
They were sent a letter
On nous a montré le jardin
We were shown the garden
On m'a dit que ...
I was told that ...

3 Ils se vendent 30 francs (la) pièce
They are sold for 30 francs each
Ce mot ne s'emploie plus
This word is no longer used

The Passive (ctd.)

Conjugation of: **être aimé** *to be liked*

PRESENT
je suis aimé(e)
tu es aimé(e)
il/elle est aimé(e)

nous sommes aimé(e)s
vous êtes aimé(e)(s)
ils/elles sont aimé(e)s

IMPERFECT
j'étais aimé(e)
tu étais aimé(e)
il/elle était aimé(e)

nous étions aimé(e)s
vous étiez aimé(e)(s)
ils/elles étaient aimé(e)s

FUTURE
je serai aimé(e)
tu seras aimé(e)
il/elle sera aimé(e)

nous serons aimé(e)s
vous serez aimé(e)(s)
ils/elles seront aimé(e)s

CONDITIONAL
je serais aimé(e)
tu serais aimé(e)
il/elle serait aimé(e)

nous serions aimé(e)s
vous seriez aimé(e)(s)
ils/elles seraient aimé(e)s

PAST HISTORIC
je fus aimé(e)
tu fus aimé(e)
il/elle fut aimé(e)

nous fûmes aimé(e)s
vous fûtes aimé(e)(s)
ils/elles furent aimé(e)s

PRESENT SUBJUNCTIVE
je sois aimé(e)
tu sois aimé(e)
il/elle soit aimé(e)

nous soyons aimé(e)s
vous soyez aimé(e)(s)
ils/elles soient aimé(e)s

IMPERFECT SUBJUNCTIVE
je fusse aimé(e)
tu fusses aimé(e)
il/elle fût aimé(e)

nous fussions aimé(e)s
vous fussiez aimé(e)(s)
ils/elles fussent aimé(e)s

The Passive (ctd.)

Conjugation of: **être aimé** *to be liked*

PERFECT
j'ai été aimé(e)	nous avons été aimé(e)s
tu as été aimé(e)	vous avez été aimé(e)(s)
il/elle a été aimé(e)	ils/elles ont été aimé(e)s

PLUPERFECT
j'avais été aimé(e)	nous avions été aimé(e)s
tu avais été aimé(e)	vous aviez été aimé(e)(s)
il/elle avait été aimé(e)	ils/elles avaient été aimé(e)s

FUTURE PERFECT
j'aurai été aimé(e)	nous aurons été aimé(e)s
tu auras été aimé(e)	vous aurez été aimé(e)(s)
il/elle aura été aimé(e)	ils/elles auront été aimé(e)s

CONDITIONAL PERFECT
j'aurais été aimé(e)	nous aurions été aimé(e)s
tu aurais été aimé(e)	vous auriez été aimé(e)s
il/elle aurait été aimé(e)	ils/elles auraient été aimé(e)s

PAST ANTERIOR
j'eus été aimé(e)	nous eûmes été aimé(e)s
tu eus été aimé(e)	vous eûtes été aimé(e)(s)
il/elle eut été aimé(e)	ils/elles eurent été aimé(e)s

PERFECT SUBJUNCTIVE
j'aie été aimé(e)	nous ayons été aimé(e)s
tu aies été aimé(e)	vous ayez été aimé(e)(s)
il/elle ait été aimé(e)	ils/elles aient été aimé(e)s

PLUPERFECT SUBJUNCTIVE
j'eusse été aimé(e)	nous eussions été aimé(e)s
tu eusses été aimé(e)	vous eussiez été aimé(e)(s)
il/elle eût été aimé(e)	ils/elles eussent été aimé(e)s

Impersonal Verbs

Impersonal verbs are used only in the infinitive and in the third person singular with the subject pronoun **il**, generally translated *it*.

e.g. **il pleut**
it's raining
il est facile de dire que ...
it's easy to say that ...

The most common impersonal verbs are:

INFINITIVE	CONSTRUCTIONS
s'agir	**il s'agit de** + noun (→**1**)
	it's a question/matter of something,
	it's about something
	il s'agit de + infinitive (→**2**)
	it's a question/matter of doing; somebody must do
falloir	**il faut** + noun object (+ indirect object) (→**3**)
	(somebody) needs something, something is necessary (to somebody)
	il faut + infinitive (+ indirect object) (→**4**)
	it is necessary to do
	il faut que + subjunctive (→**5**)
	it is necessary to do, somebody must do
grêler	**il grêle**
	it's hailing
neiger	**il neige**
	it's snowing
pleuvoir	**il pleut**	(→**6**)
	it's raining
tonner	**il tonne**
	it's thundering
valoir mieux	**il vaut mieux** + infinitive (→**7**)
	it's better to do
	il vaut mieux que + subjunctive (→**8**)
	it's better to do/that somebody does

Continued

1 Il ne s'agit pas d'argent
   It isn't a question/matter of money
   De quoi s'agit-il?
   What is it about?
   Il s'agit de la vie d'une famille au début du siècle
   It's about the life of a family at the turn of the century

2 Il s'agit de faire vite
   We must act quickly

3 Il faut du courage pour faire ça
   One needs courage to do that; Courage is needed to do that
   Il me faut une chaise de plus
   I need an extra chair

4 Il faut partir
   It is necessary to leave; We/I/You must leave*
   Il me fallait prendre une décision
   I had to make a decision

5 Il faut que vous partiez
   You have to leave/You must leave
   Il faudrait que je fasse mes valises
   I should have to/ought to pack my cases

6 Il pleuvait à verse
   It was raining heavily/It was pouring

7 Il vaut mieux refuser
   It's better to refuse; You/He/I had better refuse*
   Il vaudrait mieux rester
   You/We/She had better stay*

8 Il vaudrait mieux que nous ne venions pas
   It would be better if we didn't come; We'd better not come

   The translation here obviously depends on context

Impersonal Verbs (ctd.)

The following verbs are also commonly used in impersonal constructions:

INFINITIVE	CONSTRUCTIONS
avoir	**il y a** + noun (→1)
	there is/are
être	**il est** + noun (→2)
	it is; there are (very literary style)
	il est + adjective + **de** + infinitive (→3)
	it is
faire	**il fait** + adjective of weather (→4)
	it is
	il fait + noun depicting weather/dark/light etc.
	it is (→5)
manquer	**il manque** + noun (+ indirect object) (→6)
	there is/are … missing, something is missing/lacking
paraître	**il paraît que** + subjunctive (→7)
	it seems/appears that
	il paraît + indirect object + **que** + indicative (→8)
	it seems/appears to somebody that
rester	**il reste** + noun (+ indirect object) (→9)
	there is/are … left, (somebody) has something left
sembler	**il semble que** + subjunctive (→10)
	it seems/appears that
	il semble + indirect object + **que** + indicative (→11)
	it seems/appears to somebody that
suffire	**il suffit de** + infinitive (→12)
	it is enough to do
	il suffit de + noun (→13)
	something is enough, it only takes something

Continued

1 **Il y a du pain (qui reste)**
There is some bread (left)
Il n'y avait pas de lettres ce matin
There were no letters this morning

2 **Il est dix heures**
It's ten o'clock
Il est des gens qui …
There are (some) people who …

3 **Il était inutile de protester**
It was useless to protest
Il est facile de critiquer
Criticizing is easy

4 **Il fait beau/mauvais**
It's lovely/horrible weather

5 **Il faisait du soleil/du vent**
It was sunny/windy
Il fait jour/nuit
It's light/dark

6 **Il manque deux tasses**
There are two cups missing; Two cups are missing
Il manquait un bouton à sa chemise
His shirt had a button missing

7 **Il paraît qu'ils partent demain**
It appears they are leaving tomorrow

8 **Il nous paraît certain qu'il aura du succès**
It seems certain to us that he'll be successful

9 **Il reste deux miches de pain**
There are two loaves left
Il lui restait cinquante francs
He/She had fifty francs left

10 **Il semble que vous ayez raison**
It seems that you are right

11 **Il me semblait qu'il conduisait trop vite**
It seemed to me (that) he was driving too fast

12 **Il suffit de téléphoner pour réserver une place**
You need only phone to reserve a seat

13 **Il suffit d'une seule erreur pour tout gâcher**
One single error is enough to ruin everything

The Infinitive

The infinitive is the form of the verb found in dictionary entries meaning 'to . . .', e.g. **donner** *to give*, **vivre** *to live*.

There are three main types of verbal construction involving the infinitive:

> – with no linking preposition (→**1**)
> – with the linking preposition **à** (→**2**)
>   (see also p. 64)
> – with the linking preposition **de** (→**3**)
>   (see also p. 64)

Verbs followed by an infinitive with no linking preposition

- **devoir, pouvoir, savoir, vouloir** and **falloir** (i.e. modal auxiliary verbs: p. 52) (→**1**)
- **valoir mieux**: see Impersonal Verbs, p. 40
- verbs of seeing or hearing e.g. **voir** *to see*, **entendre** *to hear* (→**4**)
- intransitive verbs of motion e.g. **aller** *to go*, **descendre** *to come/go down* (→**5**)
- **envoyer** *to send* (→**6**)
- **faillir** (→**7**)
- **faire** (→**8**)
- **laisser** *to let, allow* (→**9**)
- The following common verbs:

adorer	*to love*	
aimer	*to like, love*	(→**10**)
aimer mieux	*to prefer*	(→**11**)
compter	*to expect*	
désirer	*to wish, want*	(→**12**)
détester	*to hate*	(→**13**)
espérer	*to hope*	(→**14**)
oser	*to dare*	(→**15**)
préférer	*to prefer*	
sembler	*to seem*	(→**16**)
souhaiter	*to wish*	

Continued

1 Voulez-vous attendre?
Would you like to wait?

2 J'apprends à nager
I'm learning to swim

3 Essayez de venir
Try to come

4 Il nous a vus arriver   **On les entend chanter**
He saw us arriving   You can hear them singing

5 Allez voir Nicolas
Go and see Nicholas
Descends leur demander
Go down and ask them

6 Je l'ai envoyé les voir
I sent him to see them

7 J'ai failli tomber
I almost fell

8 Ne me faites pas rire!
Don't make me laugh!
J'ai fait réparer ma valise
I've had my case repaired

9 Laissez-moi passer
Let me pass

10 Il aime nous accompagner
He likes to come with us

11 J'aimerais mieux le choisir moi-même
I'd rather choose it myself

12 Elle ne désire pas venir
She doesn't wish to come

13 Je déteste me lever le matin
I hate getting up in the morning

14 Espérez-vous aller en vacances?
Are you hoping to go on holiday?

15 Nous n'avons pas osé y retourner
We haven't dared go back

16 Vous semblez être inquiet
You seem to be worried

The Infinitive: Set Expressions

The following are set in French with the meaning shown:

aller chercher	*to go for, to go and get*	(→**1**)
envoyer chercher	*to send for*	(→**2**)
entendre dire que	*to hear it said that*	(→**3**)
entendre parler de	*to hear of/about*	(→**4**)
faire entrer	*to show in*	(→**5**)
faire sortir	*to let out*	(→**6**)
faire venir	*to send for*	(→**7**)
laisser tomber	*to drop*	(→**8**)
vouloir dire	*to mean*	(→**9**)

The Perfect Infinitive

● The perfect infinitive is formed using the auxiliary verb **avoir** or **être** as appropriate with the past participle of the verb (→**10**)

● The perfect infinitive is found:
  – following the preposition **après** *after* (→**11**)
  – following certain verbal constructions (→**12**)

1 **Va chercher tes photos**
   Go and get your photos
   Il est allé chercher Alexandre
   He's gone to get Alexander

2 **J'ai envoyé chercher un médecin**
   I've sent for a doctor

3 **J'ai entendu dire qu'il est malade**
   I've heard it said that he's ill

4 **Je n'ai plus entendu parler de lui**
   I didn't hear anything more (said) of him

5 **Fais entrer nos invités**
   Show our guests in

6 **J'ai fait sortir le chat**
   I've let the cat out

7 **Je vous ai fait venir parce que ...**
   I sent for you because ...

8 **Il a laissé tomber le vase**
   He dropped the vase

9 **Qu'est-ce que cela veut dire?**
   What does that mean?

10 **avoir fini**
   to have finished
   être allé   **s'être levé**
   to have gone   to have got up

11 **Après avoir pris cette décision, il nous a appelé**
   After making/having made that decision, he called us
   Après être sorties, elles se sont dirigées vers le parking
   After leaving/having left, they headed for the car park
   Après nous être levé(e)s, nous avons lu les journaux
   After getting up/having got up, we read the papers

12 **pardonner à qn d'avoir fait**
   to forgive sb for doing/having done
   remercier qn d'avoir fait
   to thank sb for doing/having done
   regretter d'avoir fait
   to be sorry for doing/having done

The Present Participle

Formation

- 1st conjugation
  Replace the **-er** of the infinitive by **-ant** (→1)

  - Verbs ending in **-cer**: **c** changes to **ç** (→2)
  - Verbs ending in **-ger**: **g** changes to **ge** (→3)

- 2nd conjugation
  Replace the **-ir** of the infinitive by **-issant** (→4)

- 3rd conjugation
  Replace the **-re** of the infinitive by **-ant** (→5)

- For irregular present participles, see irregular verbs, p. 74 ff.

Uses

The present participle has a more restricted use in French than in English.

- Used as a verbal form, the present participle is invariable. It is found:
  - on its own, where it corresponds to the English present participle (→6)
  - following the preposition **en** (→7)
  Note, in particular, the construction:
  verb + **en** + present participle
  which is often translated by an English phrasal verb, i.e. one followed by a preposition like *to run down, to bring up* (→8)

- Used as an adjective, the present participle agrees in number and gender with the noun or pronoun (→9)

- Note, in particular, the use of **ayant** and **étant** – the present participles of the auxiliary verbs **avoir** and **être** – with a past participle (→10)

Continued

1 donner → donnant
   to give   giving
2 lancer → lançant
   to throw   throwing
3 manger → mangeant
   to eat   eating
4 finir → finissant
   to finish   finishing
5 vendre → vendant
   to sell   selling
6 David, habitant près de Paris, a la possibilité de …
   David, living near Paris, has the opportunity of …
   Elle, pensant que je serais fâché, a dit '…'
   She, thinking that I would be angry, said '…'
   Ils m'ont suivi, criant à tue-tête
   They followed me, shouting at the top of their voices
7 En attendant sa sœur, Richard s'est endormi
   While waiting for his sister, Richard fell asleep
   Téléphone-nous en arrivant chez toi
   Telephone us when you get home
   En appuyant sur ce bouton, on peut …
   By pressing this button, you can …
   Il s'est blessé en essayant de sauver un chat
   He hurt himself trying to rescue a cat
8 sortir en courant
   to run out (*literally: to go out running*)
   avancer en boîtant
   to limp along (*literally: to go forward limping*)
9 le soleil couchant   **une lumière éblouissante**
   the setting sun   a dazzling light
   ils sont déroutants   **elles étaient étonnantes**
   they are disconcerting   they were surprising
10 Ayant mangé plus tôt, il a pu …
   Having eaten earlier, he was able to …
   Etant arrivée en retard, elle a dû …
   Having arrived late, she had to …

Past Participle Agreement

Like adjectives, a past participle must sometimes agree in number and gender with a noun or pronoun. For the rules of agreement, see below.
Example: **donné**

	MASCULINE	FEMININE
SING.	donné	donnée
PLUR.	donnés	données

● When the masculine singular form already ends in **-s**, no further **s** is added in the masculine plural, e.g. **pris** taken

Rules of Agreement in Compound Tenses

● When the auxiliary verb is **avoir**
The past participle remains in the masculine singular form, unless a direct object precedes the verb. The past participle then agrees in number and gender with the preceding direct object (→**1**)

● When the auxiliary verb is **être**
The past participle of a non-reflexive verb agrees in number and gender with the subject (→**2**)
The past participle of a reflexive verb agrees in number and gender with the reflexive pronoun, if the pronoun is a direct object (→**3**)
No agreement is made if the reflexive pronoun is an indirect object (→**4**)

The Past Participle as an adjective

The past participle agrees in number and gender with the noun or pronoun (→**5**)

1 Voici le livre que vous avez demandé
Here's the book you asked for
Laquelle avaient-elles choisie?
Which one had they chosen?
Ces amis? Je les ai rencontrés à Edimbourg
Those friends? I met them in Edinburgh
Il a gardé toutes les lettres qu'elle a écrites
He has kept all the letters she wrote

2 Est-ce que ton frère est allé à l'étranger?
Did your brother go abroad?
Elle était restée chez elle
She had stayed at home
Ils sont partis dans la matinée
They left in the morning
Mes cousines sont revenues hier
My cousins came back yesterday

3 Tu t'es rappelé d'acheter du pain, Georges?
Did you remember to buy bread, George?
Martine s'est demandée pourquoi il l'appelait
Martine wondered why he was calling her
'Lui et moi nous nous sommes cachés' a-t-elle dit
'He and I hid,' she said
Les vendeuses se sont mises en grève
Shop assistants have gone on strike
Vous vous êtes brouillés?
Have you fallen out with each other?
Les ouvrières s'étaient entraidées
The workers had helped one another

4 Elle s'est lavé les mains
She washed her hands
Ils se sont parlé pendant des heures
They talked to each other for hours

5 à un moment donné   **la porte ouverte**
at a given time   the open door
ils sont bien connus   **elles semblent fatiguées**
they are well-known   they seem tired

Modal Auxiliary Verbs

● In French, the modal auxiliary verbs are: **devoir**, **pouvoir**, **savoir**, **vouloir** and **falloir**.

● They are followed by a verb in the infinitive and have the following meanings:

devoir
    to have to, must (→1)
    to be due to (→2)
    in the conditional/conditional perfect:
    should/should have, ought/ought to have (→3)

pouvoir
    to be able to, can (→4)
    to be allowed to, can, may (→5)
    indicating possibility: *may/might/could* (→6)

savoir
    to know how to, can (→7)

vouloir
    to want/wish to (→8)
    to be willing to, will (→9)
    in polite phrases (→10)

falloir
    to be necessary: see Impersonal Verbs, p. 40

1 Je dois leur rendre visite
I must visit them
Elle a dû partir
She (has) had to leave
Il a dû regretter d'avoir parlé
He must have been sorry he spoke

2 Vous devez revenir demain
You're due (to come) back tomorrow
Je devais attraper le train de neuf heures mais ...
I was (supposed) to catch the nine o'clock train but ...

3 Je devrais le faire
I ought to do it
J'aurais dû m'excuser
I ought to have apologised

4 Il ne peut pas lever le bras
He can't raise his arm
Pouvez-vous réparer cette montre?
Can you mend this watch?

5 Puis-je les accompagner?
May I go with them?

6 Il peut encore changer d'avis
He may change his mind yet
Cela pourrait être vrai
It could/might be true

7 Savez-vous conduire?
Can you drive?
Je ne sais pas faire une omelette
I don't know how to make an omelette

8 Elle veut rester encore un jour
She wants to stay another day

9 Ils ne voulaient pas le faire
They wouldn't do it/They weren't willing to do it
Ma voiture ne veut pas démarrer
My car won't start

10 Voulez-vous boire quelque chose?
Would you like something to drink?

Use of Tenses

The Present

- Unlike English, French does not distinguish between the simple present (e.g. *I smoke, he reads,* we live) and the continuous present (e.g. *I am smoking, he is reading, we are living*) (→ **1**)
- To emphasise continuity, the following constructions may be used:

  être en train de faire } *to be doing* (→ **2**)
  être à faire

- French uses the present tense where English uses the perfect in the following cases:
  - with certain prepositions of time – notably **depuis** *for/since* – when an action begun in the past is continued in the present (→ **3**)
    Note, however, that the perfect is used as in English when the verb is negative or the action has been completed (→ **4**)
  - in the construction **venir de faire** *to have just done* (→ **5**)

The Future

The future is generally used as in English, but note the following:

- Immediate future time is often expressed by means of the present tense of **aller** plus an infinitive (→ **6**)
- In time clauses expressing future action, French uses the future where English uses the present (→ **7**)

The Future Perfect

- Used as in English to mean *shall/will have done* (→ **8**)
- In time clauses expressing future action, where English uses the perfect tense (→ **9**)

Continued

1 Je fume   I smoke OR I am smoking
   Il lit   He reads OR He is reading
   Nous habitons   We live OR We are living
2 Il est en train de travailler
   He's (busy) working
3 Paul apprend à nager depuis six mois
   Paul's been learning to swim for six months (*and still is*)
   Je suis debout depuis sept heures
   I've been up since seven
   Il y a longtemps que vous attendez?
   Have you been waiting long?
   Voilà deux semaines que nous sommes ici
   That's two weeks we've been here (now)
4 Ils ne se sont pas vus depuis des mois
   They haven't seen each other for months
   Elle est revenue il y a un an
   She came back a year ago
5 Elisabeth vient de partir
   Elizabeth has just left
6 Tu vas tomber si tu ne fais pas attention
   You'll fall if you're not careful
   Il va manquer le train
   He's going to miss the train
   Ça va prendre une demi-heure
   It'll take half an hour
7 Quand il viendra vous serez en vacances
   When he comes you'll be on holiday
   Faites-nous savoir aussitôt qu'elle arrivera
   Let us know as soon as she arrives
8 J'aurai fini dans une heure
   I shall have finished in an hour
9 Quand tu auras lu ce roman, rends-le-moi
   When you've read the novel, give it back to me
   Je partirai dès que j'aurai fini
   I'll leave as soon as I've finished

Use of Tenses (ctd.)

The Imperfect

- The imperfect describes:
  - an action (or state) in the past without definite limits in time (→ **1**)
  - habitual action(s) in the past (often translated by means of *would* or *used to*) (→ **2**)
- French uses the imperfect tense where English uses the pluperfect in the following cases:
  - with certain prepositions of time – notably **depuis** *for/ since* – when an action begun in the remoter past was continued in the more recent past (→ **3**)
    Note, however, that the pluperfect *is* used as in English, when the verb is negative or the action has been completed (→ **4**)
  - in the construction **venir de faire** *to have just done* (→ **5**)

The Perfect

- The perfect is used to recount a completed action or event in the past. Note that this corresponds to a perfect tense or a simple past tense in English (→ **6**)

The Past Historic

- Only ever used in *written, literary* French, the past historic recounts a completed action in the past, corresponding to a simple past tense in English (→ **7**)

The Past Anterior

This tense is used instead of the pluperfect when a verb in another part of the sentence is in the past historic. That is

- in time clauses, after conjunctions like: **quand**, **lorsque** *when*, **dès que**, **aussitôt que** *as soon as*, **après que** *after* (→ **8**)
- after **à peine** *hardly, scarcely* (→ **9**)

The Subjunctive

- In spoken French, the present subjunctive generally replaces the imperfect subjunctive. See also pp. 58 ff.

1 Elle regardait par la fenêtre
   She was looking out of the window
   Il pleuvait quand je suis sorti de chez moi
   It was raining when I left the house
   Nos chambres donnaient sur la plage
   Our rooms overlooked the beach

2 Dans sa jeunesse il se levait à l'aube
   In his youth he got up at dawn
   Nous causions des heures entières
   We would talk for hours on end
   Elle te taquinait, n'est-ce pas?
   She used to tease you, didn't she?

3 Nous habitions à Londres depuis deux ans
   We had been living in London for two years (*and still were*)
   Il était malade depuis 1985
   He had been ill since 1985
   Il y avait assez longtemps qu'il le faisait
   He had been doing it for quite a long time

4 Voilà un an que je ne l'avais pas vu
   I hadn't seen him for a year
   Il y avait une heure qu'elle était arrivée
   She had arrived one hour before

5 Je venais de les rencontrer
   I had just met them

6 Nous sommes allés au bord de la mer
   We went/have been to the seaside
   Il a refusé de nous aider
   He (has) refused to help us
   La voiture ne s'est pas arrêtée
   The car didn't stop/hasn't stopped

7 Le roi mourut en 1592
   The king died in 1592

8 Quand il eut fini, il se leva
   When he had finished, he got up

9 A peine eut-il parlé qu'on frappa à la porte
   He had scarcely spoken when there was a knock at the door

The Subjunctive: when to use it

(For how to form the subjunctive see pp. 6 ff.)

● After certain conjunctions

quoique bien que	*although* (→ **1**)
pour que afin que	*so that* (→ **2**)
pourvu que	*provided that* (→ **3**)
jusqu'à ce que	*until* (→ **4**)
avant que (... ne)	*before* (→ **5**)
à moins que (... ne)	*unless* (→ **6**)
de peur que (... ne) de crainte que (... ne)	*for fear that, lest* (→ **7**)

Note that the **ne** following the conjunctions in examples 5 to 7 has no translation value. It is often omitted in spoken informal French.

● After the conjunctions

de sorte que de façon que de manière que	*so that* (indicating a *purpose*) (→ **8**)

When these conjunctions introduce a *result* and not a *purpose*, the subjunctive is not used (→ **9**)

● After impersonal constructions which express necessity, possibility etc

il faut que il est nécessaire que	*it is necessary that* (→ **10**)
il est possible que	*it is possible that* (→ **11**)
il semble que	*it seems that* (→ **12**)
il vaut mieux que	*it is better that* (→ **13**)
il est dommage que	*it's a pity that* (→ **14**)

Continued

1 Bien qu'il fasse beaucoup d'efforts, il est peu récompensé
Although he makes a lot of effort, he isn't rewarded for it

2 Demandez un reçu afin que vous puissiez être remboursé
Ask for a receipt so that you can get a refund

3 Nous partirons ensemble pourvu que Sylvie soit d'accord
We'll leave together provided Sylvie agrees

4 Reste ici jusqu'à ce que nous revenions
Stay here until we come back

5 Je le ferai avant que tu ne partes
I'll do it before you leave

6 Ce doit être Paul, à moins que je ne me trompe
That must be Paul, unless I'm mistaken

7 Parlez bas de peur qu'on ne vous entende
Speak softly lest anyone hears you

8 Retournez-vous de sorte que je vous voie
Turn round so that I can see you

9 Il refuse de le faire de sorte que je dois le faire moi-même
He refuses to do it so that I have to do it myself

10 Il faut que je vous parle immédiatement
I must speak to you right away/It is necessary that I speak ...

11 Il est possible qu'ils aient raison
They may be right/It's possible that they are right

12 Il semble qu'elle ne soit pas venue
It appears that she hasn't come

13 Il vaut mieux que vous restiez chez vous
It's better that you stay at home

14 Il est dommage qu'elle ait perdu cette adresse
It's a shame/a pity that she's lost the address

The Subjunctive: when to use it (ctd.)

● After verbs of:
– 'wishing'

vouloir que
désirer que } *to wish that, want* (→ 1)
souhaiter que

– 'fearing'

craindre que
avoir peur que } *to be afraid that* (→ 2)

Note that **ne** in the first phrase of example 2 has no translation value. It is often omitted in spoken informal French.

– 'ordering', 'forbidding', 'allowing'

ordonner que *to order that* (→ 3)
défendre que *to forbid that* (→ 4)
permettre que *to allow that* (→ 5)

– opinion, expressing uncertainty

croire que
penser que } *to think that* (→ 6)
douter que *to doubt that* (→ 7)

– emotion (e.g. regret, shame, pleasure)

regretter que *to be sorry that* (→ 8)
être content/surpris etc **que**
to be pleased/ surprised etc *that* (→ 9)

● After a superlative (→ 10)

● After certain adjectives expressing some sort of 'uniqueness'

dernier ... qui/que *last ... who/that*
premier ... qui/que *first ... who/that*
meilleur ... qui/que *best ... who/that* } (→ 11)
seul
unique } ... **qui/que** *only ... who/that*

Continued

1 Nous voulons qu'elle soit contente
We want her to be happy (*literally: We want that she is happy*)
Désirez-vous que je le fasse?
Do you want me to do it?

2 Il craint qu'il ne soit trop tard
He's afraid it may be too late
Avez-vous peur qu'il ne revienne pas?
Are you afraid that he won't come back?

3 Il a ordonné qu'ils soient désormais à l'heure
He has ordered that they be on time from now on

4 Elle défend que vous disiez cela
She forbids you to say that

5 Permettez que nous vous aidions
Allow us to help you

6 Je ne pense pas qu'ils soient venus
I don't think they came

7 Nous doutons qu'il ait dit la vérité
We doubt that he told the truth

8 Je regrette que vous ne puissiez pas venir
I'm sorry that you cannot come

9 Je suis content que vous les aimiez
I'm pleased that you like them

10 la personne la plus sympathique que je connaisse
the nicest person I know
l'article le moins cher que j'aie jamais acheté
the cheapest item I have ever bought

11 Voici la dernière lettre qu'elle m'ait écrite
This is the last letter she wrote to me
David est la seule personne qui puisse me conseiller
David is the only person who can advise me

The Subjunctive: when to use it (ctd.)

● After
si (...) que	*however (...)*	(→ 1)
qui que	*whoever*	(→ 2)
quoi que	*whatever*	(→ 3)

  ● After **que** in the following:
    – to form the 3rd person imperative or to express a wish (→ 4)
    – when **que** has the meaning *if*, replacing **si** in a clause (→ 5)
    – when **que** has the meaning *whether* (→ 6)

● In relative clauses following certain types of indefinite and negative construction (→ 7/8)

● In set expressions (→ 9)

1 si courageux qu'il soit
however brave he may be
si peu que ce soit
however little it is

2 Qui que vous soyez, allez-vous-en!
Whoever you are, go away!

3 Quoi que nous fassions, ...
Whatever we do, ...

4 Qu'il entre!
Let him come in!
Que cela vous serve de leçon!
Let that be a lesson to you!

5 S'il fait beau et que tu te sentes mieux, nous irons ...
If it's nice and you're feeling better, we'll go ...

6 Que tu viennes ou non, je ...
Whether you come or not, I ...

7 Il cherche une maison qui ait deux caves
He's looking for a house which has two cellars
(*subjunctive used since such a house may or may not exist*)
J'ai besoin d'un livre qui décrive l'art du mime
I need a book which describes the art of mime
(*subjunctive used since such a book may or may not exist*)

8 Je n'ai rencontré personne qui la connaisse
I haven't met anyone who knows her
Il n'y a rien qui puisse vous empêcher de ...
There's nothing that can prevent you from ...

9 Vive le roi!
Long live the king!
Que Dieu vous bénisse!
God bless you!

Verbs governing à and de

The following lists (pp. 64 to 72) contain common verbal constructions using the prepositions **à** and **de**

Note the following abbreviations:

infin.	infinitive
perf. infin.	perfect infinitive*
qch	quelque chose
qn	quelqu'un
sb	sómebody
sth	something

*For formation see p. 46

accuser qn de qch/de + perf. infin.	to accuse sb of sth/of doing, having done (→ **1**)
accoutumer qn à qch/à + infin.	to accustom sb to sth/to doing
acheter qch à qn	to buy sth from sb/for sb (→ **2**)
achever de + infin.	to end up doing
aider qn à + infin.	to help sb to do (→ **3**)
s'amuser à + infin.	to have fun doing
s'apercevoir de qch	to notice sth (→ **4**)
apprendre qch à qn	to teach sb sth
apprendre à + infin.	to learn to do (→ **5**)
apprendre à qn à + infin.	to teach sb to do (→ **6**)
s'approcher de qn/qch	to approach sb/sth (→ **7**)
arracher qch à qn	to snatch sth from sb (→ **8**)
(s')arrêter de + infin.	to stop doing (→ **9**)
arriver à + infin.	to manage to do (→ **10**)
assister à qch	to attend sth, be at sth
s'attendre à + infin.	to expect to do (→ **11**)
blâmer qn de qch/de + perf. infin.	to blame sb for sth/for having done (→ **12**)
cacher qch à qn	to hide sth from sb (→ **13**)
cesser de + infin.	to stop doing (→ **14**)

Continued

1 Il m'a accusé d'avoir menti
He accused me of lying

2 Marie-Christine leur a acheté deux billets
Marie-Christine bought two tickets from/for them

3 Aidez-moi à porter ces valises
Help me to carry these cases

4 Il ne s'est pas aperçu de son erreur
He didn't notice his mistake

5 Elle apprend à lire
She's learning to read

6 Je lui apprends à nager
I'm teaching him/her to swim

7 Elle s'est approchée de moi, en disant '…'
She came up to me, saying '…'

8 Le voleur lui a arraché l'argent
The thief snatched the money from him/her

9 Arrêtez de faire du bruit!
Stop being (so) noisy!

10 Je n'arrive pas à le comprendre
I can't understand it

11 Est-ce qu'elle s'attendait à le voir?
Was she expecting to see him?

12 Je ne la blâme pas de l'avoir fait
I don't blame her for doing it

13 Cache-les-leur!
Hide them from them!

14 Est-ce qu'il a cessé de pleuvoir?
Has it stopped raining?

Verbs governing à and de (ctd.)

changer de qch	*to change sth* (→ **1**)
se charger de qch/de + infin.	*to see to sth/undertake to do*
chercher à + infin.	*to try to do*
commander à qn de + infin.	*to order sb to do* (→ **2**)
commencer à/de + infin.	*to begin to do* (→ **3**)
conseiller à qn de + infin.	*to advise sb to do* (→ **4**)
consentir à qch/à + infin.	*to agree to sth/to do* (→ **5**)
continuer à/de + infin.	*to continue to do*
craindre de + infin.	*to be afraid to do/of doing*
décider de + infin.	*to decide to do* (→ **6**)
se décider à + infin.	*to make up one's mind to do*
défendre à qn de + infin.	*to forbid sb to do* (→ **7**)
demander qch à qn	*to ask sb sth/for sth* (→ **8**)
demander à qn de + infin.	*to ask sb to do* (→ **9**)
se dépêcher de + infin.	*to hurry to do*
dépendre de qn/qch	*to depend on sb/sth*
déplaire à qn	*to displease sb* (→ **10**)
désobéir à qn	*to disobey sb* (→ **11**)
dire à qn de + infin.	*to tell sb to do* (→ **12**)
dissuader qn de + infin.	*to dissuade sb from doing*
douter de qch	*to doubt sth*
se douter de qch	*to suspect sth*
s'efforcer de + infin.	*to strive to do*
empêcher qn de + infin.	*to prevent sb from doing* (→ **13**)
emprunter qch à qn	*to borrow sth from sb* (→ **14**)
encourager qn à + infin.	*to encourage sb to do* (→ **15**)
enlever qch à qn	*to take sth away from sb*
enseigner qch à qn	*to teach sb sth*
enseigner à qn à + infin.	*to teach sb to do*
entreprendre de + infin.	*to undertake to do*
essayer de + infin.	*to try to do* (→ **16**)
éviter de + infin.	*to avoid doing* (→ **17**)

Continued

1 J'ai changé d'avis/de robe
I changed my mind/my dress
Il faut changer de train à Toulouse
You have to change trains at Toulouse

2 Il leur a commandé de tirer
He ordered them to shoot

3 Il commence à neiger
It's starting to snow

4 Il leur a conseillé d'attendre
He advised them to wait

5 Je n'ai pas consenti à l'aider
I haven't agreed to help him/her

6 Qu'est-ce que vous avez décidé de faire?
What have you decided to do?

7 Je leur ai défendu de sortir
I've forbidden them to go out

8 Je lui ai demandé l'heure
I asked him/her the time
Il lui a demandé un livre
He asked him/her for a book

9 Demande à Alain de le faire
Ask Alan to do it

10 Leur attitude lui déplaît
He/She doesn't like their attitude

11 Ils lui désobéissent souvent
They often disobey him/her

12 Dites-leur de se taire
Tell them to be quiet

13 Le bruit m'empêche de travailler
The noise is preventing me from working

14 Puis-je vous emprunter ce stylo?
May I borrow this pen from you?

15 Elle encourage ses enfants à être indépendants
She encourages her children to be independent

16 Essayez d'arriver à l'heure
Try to arrive on time

17 Il évite de lui parler
He avoids speaking to him/her

Verbs governing à and de (ctd.)

s'excuser de qch/de + (perf.) infin.	to apologise for sth/for doing, having done (→ **1**)
exceller à + infin.	to excel at doing
se fâcher de qch	to be annoyed at sth
feindre de + infin.	to pretend to do (→ **2**)
féliciter qn de qch/de + (perf.) infin.	to congratulate sb on sth/on doing, having done (→ **3**)
se fier à qn	to trust sb (→ **4**)
finir de + infin.	to finish doing (→ **5**)
forcer qn à + infin.	to force sb to do
habituer qn à + infin.	to accustom sb to doing
s'habituer à + infin.	to get/be used to doing (→ **6**)
se hâter de + infin.	to hurry to do
hésiter à + infin.	to hesitate to do
interdire à qn de + infin.	to forbid sb to do (→ **7**)
s'intéresser à qn/qch/à + infin.	to be interested in sb/sth/in doing (→ **8**)
inviter qn à + infin.	to invite sb to do (→ **9**)
jouer à (+ sports, games)	to play (→ **10**)
jouer de (+ musical instruments)	to play (→ **11**)
jouir de qch	to enjoy sth (→ **12**)
jurer de + infin.	to swear to do
louer qn de qch	to praise sb for sth
manquer à qn	to be missed by sb (→ **13**)
manquer de qch	to lack sth
manquer de + infin.	to fail to do (→ **14**)
se marier à qn	to marry sb
se méfier de qn	to distrust sb
menacer de + infin.	to threaten to do (→ **15**)
mériter de + infin.	to deserve to do (→ **16**)
se mettre à + infin.	to begin to do
se moquer de qn/qch	to make fun of sb/sth
négliger de + infin.	to fail to do

Continued

1 **Je m'excuse d'être (arrivé) en retard**
  I apologise for being (arriving) late
2 **Elle feint de dormir**
  She's pretending to be asleep
3 **Je l'ai félicitée d'avoir gagné**
  I congratulated her on winning
4 **Je ne me fie pas à ces gens-là**
  I don't trust those people
5 **Avez-vous fini de lire ce journal?**
  Have you finished reading this newspaper?
6 **Il s'est habitué à boire moins de café**
  He got used to drinking less coffee
7 **Il a interdit aux enfants de jouer avec des allumettes**
  He's forbidden the children to play with matches
8 **Elle s'intéresse beaucoup au sport**
  She's very interested in sport
9 **Il m'a invitée à danser**
  He asked me to dance
10 **Elle joue au tennis et au hockey**
  She plays tennis and hockey
11 **Il joue du piano et de la guitare**
  He plays the piano and the guitar
12 **Il jouit d'une santé solide**
  He enjoys good health
13 **Tu manques à tes parents**
  Your parents miss you
14 **Je ne manquerai pas de le lui dire**
  I'll be sure to tell him/her about it
15 **Elle a menacé de démissionner tout de suite**
  She threatened to resign at once
16 **Ils méritent d'être promus**
  They deserve to be promoted

Verbs governing à and de (ctd.)

nuire à qch	*to harm sth* (→ **1**)
obéir à qn	*to obey sb*
obliger qn **à** + infin.	*to oblige sb to do* (→ **2**)
s'occuper de qch/qn	*to look after sth/sb* (→ **3**)
offrir de + infin.	*to offer to do* (→ **4**)
omettre de + infin.	*to fail to do*
ordonner à qn **de** + infin.	*to order sb to do* (→ **5**)
ôter qch **à** qn	*to take sth away from sb*
oublier de + infin.	*to forget to do*
pardonner qch **à** qn	*to forgive sb for sth*
pardonner à qn **de** + perf. infin.	*to forgive sb for having done* (→ **6**)
parvenir à + infin.	*to manage to do*
se passer de qch	*to do/go without do* (→ **7**)
penser à qn/qch	*to think about sb/sth* (→ **8**)
permettre qch **à** qn	*to allow sb sth*
permettre à qn **de** + infin.	*to allow sb to do* (→ **9**)
persister à + infin.	*to persist in doing*
persuader qn **de** + infin.	*to persuade sb to do* (→ **10**)
se plaindre de qch	*to complain about sth*
plaire à qn	*to please sb* (→ **11**)
pousser qn **à** + infin.	*to urge sb to do*
prendre qch **à** qn	*to take sth from sb* (→ **12**)
préparer qn **à** + infin.	*to prepare sb to do*
se préparer à + infin.	*to get ready to do*
prier qn **de** + infin.	*to beg sb to do*
profiter de qch/**de** + infin.	*to take advantage of sth/of doing*
promettre à qn **de** + infin.	*to promise sb to do* (→ **13**)
proposer de + infin.	*to suggest doing* (→ **14**)
punir qn **de** qch	*to punish sb for sth* (→ **15**)
récompenser qn **de** qch	*to reward sb for sth*
réfléchir à qch	*to think about sth*
refuser de + infin.	*to refuse to do* (→ **16**)

Continued

1 **Ce mode de vie va nuire à sa santé**
This lifestyle will damage her health

2 **Il les a obligés à faire la vaisselle**
He made them do the washing-up

3 **Je m'occupe de ma nièce**
I'm looking after my niece

4 **Stuart a offert de nous accompagner**
Stuart has offered to go with us

5 **Les soldats leur ont ordonné de se rendre**
The soldiers ordered them to give themselves up

6 **Est-ce que tu as pardonné à Charles de t'avoir menti?**
Have you forgiven Charles for lying to you?

7 **Nous nous sommes passés d'électricité pendant plusieurs jours**
We did without electricity for several days

8 **Je pense souvent à toi**
I often think about you

9 **Permettez-moi de continuer, s'il vous plaît**
Allow me to go on, please

10 **Elle nous a persuadés de rester**
She persuaded us to stay

11 **Est-ce que ce genre de film lui plaît?**
Does he/she like this kind of film?

12 **Je lui ai pris son baladeur**
I took his personal stereo from him

13 **Ils ont promis à Pascale de venir**
They promised Pascale that they would come

14 **J'ai proposé de les inviter**
I suggested inviting them

15 **Il a été puni de sa malhonnêteté**
He has been punished for his dishonesty

16 **Il a refusé de coopérer**
He has refused to cooperate

Verbs governing à and de (ctd.)

regretter de + perf. infin.	to regret doing, having done (→ 1)
remercier qn de qch/de + perf. infin.	to thank sb for sth/for doing, having done (→ 2)
renoncer à qch/à + infin.	to give sth up/give up doing
reprocher qch à qn	to reproach sb with/for sth (→ 3)
résister à qch	to resist sth (→ 4)
résoudre de + infin.	to resolve to do
ressembler à qn/qch	to look/be like sb/sth (→ 5)
réussir à + infin.	to manage to do (→ 6)
rire de qn/qch	to laugh at sb/sth
risquer de + infin.	to risk doing (→ 7)
servir à qch/à + infin.	to be used for sth/for doing (→ 8)
se servir de qch	to use sth; to help oneself to sth (→ 9)
songer à + infin.	to think of doing
se souvenir de qn/qch/de + perf. infin.	to remember sb/sth/doing, having done (→ 10)
succéder à qn	to succeed sb
survivre à qn	to outlive sb (→ 11)
tâcher de + infin.	to try to do (→ 12)
tarder à + infin.	to delay doing (→ 13)
tendre à + infin.	to tend to do
tenir à + infin.	to be keen to do (→ 14)
tenter de + infin.	to try to do (→ 15)
se tromper de qch	to be wrong about sth (→ 16)
venir de* + infin.	to have just done (→ 17)
vivre de qch	to live on sth
voler qch à qn	to steal sth from sb

*See also Use of Tenses, pp. 54 and 56

1 **Je regrette de ne pas vous avoir écrit plus tôt**
I'm sorry for not writing to you sooner
2 **Nous les avons remerciés de leur gentillesse**
We thanked them for their kindness
3 **On lui reproche son manque d'enthousiasme**
They're reproaching him for his lack of enthusiasm
4 **Comment résistez-vous à la tentation?**
How do you resist temptation?
5 **Elles ressemblent beaucoup à leur mère**
They look very like their mother
6 **Vous avez réussi à me convaincre**
You've managed to convince me
7 **Vous risquez de tomber en faisant cela**
You risk falling doing that
8 **Ce bouton sert à régler le volume**
This knob is (used) for adjusting the volume
9 **Il s'est servi d'un tournevis pour l'ouvrir**
He used a screwdriver to open it
10 **Vous vous souvenez de Lucienne?**
Do you remember Lucienne?
Il ne se souvient pas de l'avoir perdu
He doesn't remember losing it
11 **Elle a survécu à son mari**
She outlived her husband
12 **Tâchez de ne pas être en retard!**
Try not to be late!
13 **Ils n'a pas tardé à prendre une décision**
He was not long in taking a decision
14 **Elle tient à le faire elle-même**
She's keen to do it herself
15 **J'ai tenté de la comprendre**
I've tried to understand her
16 **Je me suis trompé de route**
I took the wrong road
17 **Mon père vient de téléphoner** **Nous venions d'arriver**
My father's just phoned We had just arrived

Irregular Verbs

The verbs listed opposite and conjugated on pp. 76 to 131 provide the main patterns for irregular verbs. The verbs are grouped opposite according to their infinitive ending (except **avoir** and **être**), and are shown in the following tables in alphabetical order.

In the tables, the most important irregular verbs are given in their most common simple tenses, together with the imperative and the present participle.

The auxiliary (**avoir** or **être**) is also shown for each verb, together with the past participle, to enable you to form all the compound tenses, as on pp. 24 and 26.

● For a fuller list of irregular verbs, the reader is referred to Collins Gem French Verb Tables, which shows you how to conjugate some 2000 French verbs.

Continued

	avoir
	être

'-er':	aller	'-re':	battre
	envoyer		boire
			connaître
'-ir':	acquérir		coudre
	bouillir		craindre
	courir		croire
	cueillir		croître
	dormir		cuire
	fuir		dire
	haïr		écrire
	mourir		faire
	ouvrir		lire
	partir		mettre
	sentir		moudre
	servir		naître
	sortir		paraître
	tenir		plaire
	venir		prendre
	vêtir		résoudre
			rire
'-oir':	s'asseoir		rompre
	devoir		suffire
	falloir		suivre
	pleuvoir		se taire
	pouvoir		vaincre
	recevoir		vivre
	savoir		
	valoir		
	voir		
	vouloir		

acquérir *to acquire*   Auxiliary: **avoir**

PAST PARTICIPLE
acquis

IMPERATIVE
acquiers
acquérons
acquérez

PRESENT PARTICIPLE
acquérant

PRESENT
     j'acquiers
tu **acquiers**
il **acquiert**
nous **acquérons**
vous **acquérez**
ils **acquièrent**

IMPERFECT
     j'acquérais
tu **acquérais**
il **acquérait**
nous **acquérions**
vous **acquériez**
ils **acquéraient**

FUTURE
     j'acquerrai
tu **acquerras**
il **acquerra**
nous **acquerrons**
vous **acquerrez**
ils **acquerront**

CONDITIONAL
     j'acquerrais
tu **acquerrais**
il **acquerrait**
nous **acquerrions**
vous **acquerriez**
ils **acquerraient**

PRESENT SUBJUNCTIVE
     j'acquière
tu **acquières**
il **acquière**
nous **acquérions**
vous **acquériez**
ils **acquièrent**

PAST HISTORIC
     j'acquis
tu **acquis**
il **acquit**
nous **acquîmes**
vous **acquîtes**
ils **acquirent**

aller *to go*   Auxiliary: **être**

PAST PARTICIPLE
allé

IMPERATIVE
va
allons
allez

PRESENT PARTICIPLE
allant

PRESENT

je	**vais**
tu	**vas**
il	**va**
nous	allons
vous	allez
ils	**vont**

IMPERFECT

	j'allais
tu	allais
il	allait
nous	allions
vous	alliez
ils	allaient

FUTURE

	j'irai
tu	**iras**
il	**ira**
nous	**irons**
vous	**irez**
ils	**iront**

CONDITIONAL

	j'irais
tu	**irais**
il	**irait**
nous	**irions**
vous	**iriez**
ils	**iraient**

PRESENT SUBJUNCTIVE

	j'aille
tu	**ailles**
il	**aille**
nous	allions
vous	alliez
ils	**aillent**

PAST HISTORIC

	j'allai
tu	allas
il	alla
nous	allâmes
vous	allâtes
ils	allèrent

s'asseoir *to sit down*   Auxiliary: être

PAST PARTICIPLE
assis

IMPERATIVE
assieds-toi
asseyons-nous
asseyez-vous

PRESENT PARTICIPLE
s'asseyant

PRESENT		IMPERFECT	
je	m'assieds *or* assois	je	m'asseyais
tu	t'assieds *or* assois	tu	t'asseyais
il	s'assied *or* assoit	il	s'asseyait
nous	nous asseyons *or* assoyons	nous	nous asseyions
vous	vous asseyez *or* assoyez	vous	vous asseyiez
ils	s'asseyent *or* assoient	ils	s'asseyaient

FUTURE		CONDITIONAL	
je	m'assiérai	je	m'assiérais
tu	t'assiéras	tu	t'assiérais
il	s'assiéra	il	s'assiérait
nous	nous assiérons	nous	nous assiérions
vous	vous assiérez	vous	vous assiériez
ils	s'assiéront	ils	s'assiéraient

PRESENT SUBJUNCTIVE		PAST HISTORIC	
je	m'asseye	je	m'assis
tu	t'asseyes	tu	t'assis
il	s'asseye	il	s'assit
nous	nous asseyions	nous	nous assîmes
vous	vous asseyiez	vous	vous assîtes
ils	s'asseyent	ils	s'assirent

avoir *to have*   Auxiliary: **avoir**

PAST PARTICIPLE
  eu

PRESENT PARTICIPLE
  ayant

IMPERATIVE
  aie
  ayons
  ayez

PRESENT		*IMPERFECT*	
	j'ai		j'avais
tu	as	tu	avais
il	a	il	avait
nous	avons	nous	avions
vous	avez	vous	aviez
ils	ont	ils	avaient

FUTURE		*CONDITIONAL*	
	j'aurai		j'aurais
tu	auras	tu	aurais
il	aura	il	aurait
nous	aurons	nous	aurions
vous	aurez	vous	auriez
ils	auront	ils	auraient

PRESENT SUBJUNCTIVE		*PAST HISTORIC*	
	j'aie		j'eus
tu	aies	tu	eus
il	ait	il	eut
nous	ayons	nous	eûmes
vous	ayez	vous	eûtes
ils	aient	ils	eurent

battre *to beat*　　　　　　　　Auxiliary: **avoir**

PAST PARTICIPLE	IMPERATIVE
battu	**bats**
	battons
PRESENT PARTICIPLE	battez
battant	

PRESENT		IMPERFECT	
je	**bats**	je	battais
tu	**bats**	tu	battais
il	**bat**	il	battait
nous	battons	nous	battions
vous	battez	vous	battiez
ils	battent	ils	battaient

FUTURE		CONDITIONAL	
je	battrai	je	battrais
tu	battras	tu	battrais
il	battra	il	battrait
nous	battrons	nous	battrions
vous	battrez	vous	battriez
ils	battront	ils	battraient

PRESENT SUBJUNCTIVE		PAST HISTORIC	
je	batte	je	battis
tu	battes	tu	battis
il	batte	il	battit
nous	battions	nous	battîmes
vous	battiez	vous	battîtes
ils	battent	ils	battirent

boire *to drink*   Auxiliary: **avoir**

PAST PARTICIPLE	IMPERATIVE
bu	bois
	buvons
PRESENT PARTICIPLE	**buvez**
buvant	

PRESENT		IMPERFECT	
je	bois	**je**	**buvais**
tu	bois	**tu**	**buvais**
il	boit	**il**	**buvait**
nous	**buvons**	**nous**	**buvions**
vous	**buvez**	**vous**	**buviez**
ils	**boivent**	**ils**	**buvaient**

FUTURE		CONDITIONAL	
je	boirai	je	boirais
tu	boiras	tu	boirais
il	boira	il	boirait
nous	boirons	nous	boirions
vous	boirez	vous	boiriez
ils	boiront	ils	boiraient

PRESENT SUBJUNCTIVE		PAST HISTORIC	
je	**boive**	**je**	**bus**
tu	**boives**	**tu**	**bus**
il	**boive**	**il**	**but**
nous	**buvions**	**nous**	**bûmes**
vous	**buviez**	**vous**	**bûtes**
ils	**boivent**	**ils**	**burent**

bouillir *to boil*   Auxiliary: **avoir**

PAST PARTICIPLE
  bouilli

IMPERATIVE
  bous
  bouillons
  bouillez

PRESENT PARTICIPLE
  bouillant

PRESENT
je	**bous**
tu	**bous**
il	**bout**
nous	**bouillons**
vous	**bouillez**
ils	**bouillent**

IMPERFECT
je	**bouillais**
tu	**bouillais**
il	**bouillait**
nous	**bouillions**
vous	**bouilliez**
ils	**bouillaient**

FUTURE
je	bouillirai
tu	bouilliras
il	bouillira
nous	bouillirons
vous	bouillirez
ils	bouilliront

CONDITIONAL
je	bouillirais
tu	bouillirais
il	bouillirait
nous	bouillirions
vous	bouilliriez
ils	bouilliraient

PRESENT SUBJUNCTIVE
je	**bouille**
tu	**bouilles**
il	**bouille**
nous	**bouillions**
vous	**bouilliez**
ils	**bouillent**

PAST HISTORIC
je	bouillis
tu	bouillis
il	bouillit
nous	bouillîmes
vous	bouillîtes
ils	bouillirent

connaître *to know*

Auxiliary: **avoir**

PAST PARTICIPLE
connu

PRESENT PARTICIPLE
connaissant

IMPERATIVE
connais
connaissons
connaissez

PRESENT

je	**connais**
tu	**connais**
il	**connaît**
nous	**connaissons**
vous	**connaissez**
ils	**connaissent**

IMPERFECT

je	**connaissais**
tu	**connaissais**
il	**connaissait**
nous	**connaissions**
vous	**connaissiez**
ils	**connaissaient**

FUTURE

je	connaîtrai
tu	connaîtras
il	connaîtra
nous	connaîtrons
vous	connaîtrez
ils	connaîtront

CONDITIONAL

je	connaîtrais
tu	connaîtrais
il	connaîtrait
nous	connaîtrions
vous	connaîtriez
ils	connaîtraient

PRESENT SUBJUNCTIVE

je	**connaisse**
tu	**connaisses**
il	**connaisse**
nous	**connaissions**
vous	**connaissiez**
ils	**connaissent**

PAST HISTORIC

je	**connus**
tu	**connus**
il	**connut**
nous	**connûmes**
vous	**connûtes**
ils	**connurent**

coudre *to sew*   Auxiliary: **avoir**

PAST PARTICIPLE
  cousu

IMPERATIVE
  couds
  cousons
  cousez

PRESENT PARTICIPLE
  cousant

PRESENT
je	couds
tu	couds
il	coud
nous	**cousons**
vous	**cousez**
ils	**cousent**

IMPERFECT
je	**cousais**
tu	**cousais**
il	**cousait**
nous	**cousions**
vous	**cousiez**
ils	**cousaient**

FUTURE
je	coudrai
tu	coudras
il	coudra
nous	coudrons
vous	coudrez
ils	coudront

CONDITIONAL
je	coudrais
tu	coudrais
il	coudrait
nous	coudrions
vous	coudriez
ils	coudraient

PRESENT SUBJUNCTIVE
je	**couse**
tu	**couses**
il	**couse**
nous	**cousions**
vous	**cousiez**
ils	**cousent**

PAST HISTORIC
je	**cousis**
tu	**cousis**
il	**cousit**
nous	**cousîmes**
vous	**cousîtes**
ils	**cousirent**

courir *to run*   Auxiliary: **avoir**

PAST PARTICIPLE
  couru

IMPERATIVE
cours
courons
courez

PRESENT PARTICIPLE
  courant

PRESENT		*IMPERFECT*	
je	**cours**	je	**courais**
tu	**cours**	tu	**courais**
il	**court**	il	**courait**
nous	**courons**	nous	**courions**
vous	**courez**	vous	**couriez**
ils	**courent**	ils	**couraient**

FUTURE		*CONDITIONAL*	
je	**courrai**	je	**courrais**
tu	**courras**	tu	**courrais**
il	**courra**	il	**courrait**
nous	**courrons**	nous	**courrions**
vous	**courrez**	vous	**courriez**
ils	**courront**	ils	**courraient**

PRESENT SUBJUNCTIVE		*PAST HISTORIC*	
je	**coure**	je	**courus**
tu	**coures**	tu	**courus**
il	**coure**	il	**courut**
nous	**courions**	nous	**courûmes**
vous	**couriez**	vous	**courûtes**
ils	**courent**	ils	**coururent**

craindre *to fear*

Auxiliary: **avoir**

PAST PARTICIPLE
craint

PRESENT PARTICIPLE
craignant

IMPERATIVE
crains
craignons
craignez

PRESENT		*IMPERFECT*	
je	crains	je	craignais
tu	crains	tu	craignais
il	craint	il	craignait
nous	craignons	nous	craignions
vous	craignez	vous	craigniez
ils	craignent	ils	craignaient

FUTURE		*CONDITIONAL*	
je	craindrai	je	craindrais
tu	craindras	tu	craindrais
il	craindra	il	craindrait
nous	craindrons	nous	craindrions
vous	craindrez	vous	craindriez
ils	craindront	ils	craindraient

PRESENT SUBJUNCTIVE		*PAST HISTORIC*	
je	craigne	je	craignis
tu	craignes	tu	craignis
il	craigne	il	craignit
nous	craignions	nous	craignîmes
vous	craigniez	vous	craignîtes
ils	craignent	ils	craignirent

Verbs ending in **-eindre** and **-oindre** are conjugated similarly

croire *to believe*   Auxiliary: **avoir**

PAST PARTICIPLE
cru

IMPERATIVE
crois
croyons
croyez

PRESENT PARTICIPLE
croyant

PRESENT
- je crois
- tu crois
- **il croit**
- **nous croyons**
- **vous croyez**
- ils croient

IMPERFECT
- **je croyais**
- **tu croyais**
- **il croyait**
- **nous croyions**
- **vous croyiez**
- **ils croyaient**

FUTURE
- je croirai
- tu croiras
- il croira
- nous croirons
- vous croirez
- ils croiront

CONDITIONAL
- je croirais
- tu croirais
- il croirait
- nous croirions
- vous croiriez
- ils croiraient

PRESENT SUBJUNCTIVE
- je croie
- tu croies
- il croie
- **nous croyions**
- **vous croyiez**
- ils croient

PAST HISTORIC
- **je crus**
- **tu crus**
- **il crut**
- **nous crûmes**
- **vous crûtes**
- **ils crurent**

croître *to grow*   Auxiliary: **avoir**

PAST PARTICIPLE
crû

IMPERATIVE
croîs
croissons
croissez

PRESENT PARTICIPLE
croissant

PRESENT		IMPERFECT	
je	**croîs**	je	**croissais**
tu	**croîs**	tu	**croissais**
il	**croît**	il	**croissait**
nous	**croissons**	nous	**croissions**
vous	**croissez**	vous	**croissiez**
ils	**croissent**	ils	**croissaient**

FUTURE		CONDITIONAL	
je	**croîtrai**	je	**croîtrais**
tu	**croîtras**	tu	**croîtrais**
il	**croîtra**	il	**croîtrait**
nous	**croîtrons**	nous	**croîtrions**
vous	**croîtrez**	vous	**croîtriez**
ils	**croîtront**	ils	**croîtraient**

PRESENT SUBJUNCTIVE		PAST HISTORIC	
je	**croisse**	je	**crûs**
tu	**croisses**	tu	**crûs**
il	**croisse**	il	**crût**
nous	**croissions**	nous	**crûmes**
vous	**croissiez**	vous	**crûtes**
ils	**croissent**	ils	**crûrent**

cueillir *to pick*   Auxiliary: **avoir**

PAST PARTICIPLE
  cueilli

IMPERATIVE
  cueille
  cueillons
  cueillez

PRESENT PARTICIPLE
  cueillant

PRESENT		IMPERFECT	
je	**cueille**	je	**cueillais**
tu	**cueilles**	tu	**cueillais**
il	**cueille**	il	**cueillait**
nous	**cueillons**	nous	**cueillions**
vous	**cueillez**	vous	**cueilliez**
ils	**cueillent**	ils	**cueillaient**

FUTURE		CONDITIONAL	
je	**cueillerai**	je	**cueillerais**
tu	**cueilleras**	tu	**cueillerais**
il	**cueillera**	il	**cueillerait**
nous	**cueillerons**	nous	**cueillerions**
vous	**cueillerez**	vous	**cueilleriez**
ils	**cueilleront**	ils	**cueilleraient**

PRESENT SUBJUNCTIVE		PAST HISTORIC	
je	**cueille**	je	cueillis
tu	**cueilles**	tu	cueillis
il	**cueille**	il	cueillit
nous	**cueillions**	nous	cueillîmes
vous	**cueilliez**	vous	cueillîtes
ils	**cueillent**	ils	cueillirent

cuire *to cook*   Auxiliary: **avoir**

PAST PARTICIPLE
  cuit

IMPERATIVE
  cuis
  cuisons
  cuisez

PRESENT PARTICIPLE
  cuisant

PRESENT		IMPERFECT	
je	cuis	**je**	**cuisais**
tu	cuis	**tu**	**cuisais**
il	**cuit**	**il**	**cuisait**
nous	**cuisons**	**nous**	**cuisions**
vous	**cuisez**	**vous**	**cuisiez**
ils	**cuisent**	**ils**	**cuisaient**

FUTURE		CONDITIONAL	
je	cuirai	je	cuirais
tu	cuiras	tu	cuirais
il	cuira	il	cuirait
nous	cuirons	nous	cuirions
vous	cuirez	vous	cuiriez
ils	cuiront	ils	cuiraient

PRESENT SUBJUNCTIVE		PAST HISTORIC	
je	**cuise**	**je**	**cuisis**
tu	**cuises**	**tu**	**cuisis**
il	**cuise**	**il**	**cuisit**
nous	**cuisions**	**nous**	**cuisîmes**
vous	**cuisiez**	**vous**	**cuisîtes**
ils	**cuisent**	**ils**	**cuisirent**

nuire *to harm*, conjugated similarly, but past participle **nui**

devoir *to have to; to owe*   Auxiliary: **avoir**

PAST PARTICIPLE
dû

PRESENT PARTICIPLE
devant

IMPERATIVE
dois
devons
devez

PRESENT

je	**dois**
tu	**dois**
il	**doit**
nous	**devons**
vous	**devez**
ils	**doivent**

IMPERFECT

je	**devais**
tu	**devais**
il	**devait**
nous	**devions**
vous	**deviez**
ils	**devaient**

FUTURE

je	**devrai**
tu	**devras**
il	**devra**
nous	**devrons**
vous	**devrez**
ils	**devront**

CONDITIONAL

je	**devrais**
tu	**devrais**
il	**devrait**
nous	**devrions**
vous	**devriez**
ils	**devraient**

PRESENT SUBJUNCTIVE

je	**doive**
tu	**doives**
il	**doive**
nous	**devions**
vous	**deviez**
ils	**doivent**

PAST HISTORIC

je	**dus**
tu	**dus**
il	**dut**
nous	**dûmes**
vous	**dûtes**
ils	**durent**

dire *to say, tell*   Auxiliary: **avoir**

PAST PARTICIPLE
dit

PRESENT PARTICIPLE
disant

IMPERATIVE
dis
disons
dites

PRESENT		IMPERFECT	
je	dis	je	disais
tu	dis	tu	disais
il	dit	il	disait
nous	disons	nous	disions
vous	dites	vous	disiez
ils	disent	ils	disaient

FUTURE		CONDITIONAL	
je	dirai	je	dirais
tu	diras	tu	dirais
il	dira	il	dirait
nous	dirons	nous	dirions
vous	direz	vous	diriez
ils	diront	ils	diraient

PRESENT SUBJUNCTIVE		PAST HISTORIC	
je	dise	je	dis
tu	dises	tu	dis
il	dise	il	dit
nous	disions	nous	dîmes
vous	disiez	vous	dîtes
ils	disent	ils	dirent

interdire *to forbid*, conjugated similarly, but 2nd person plural of the present tense is **vous interdisez**

dormir *to sleep*   Auxiliary: **avoir**

PAST PARTICIPLE
dormi

IMPERATIVE
dors
dormons
dormez

PRESENT PARTICIPLE
dormant

PRESENT		IMPERFECT	
je	**dors**	**je**	**dormais**
tu	**dors**	**tu**	**dormais**
il	**dort**	**il**	**dormait**
nous	**dormons**	**nous**	**dormions**
vous	**dormez**	**vous**	**dormiez**
ils	**dorment**	**ils**	**dormaient**

FUTURE		CONDITIONAL	
je	dormirai	je	dormirais
tu	dormiras	tu	dormirais
il	dormira	il	dormirait
nous	dormirons	nous	dormirions
vous	dormirez	vous	dormiriez
ils	dormiront	ils	dormiraient

PRESENT SUBJUNCTIVE		PAST HISTORIC	
je	**dorme**	je	dormis
tu	**dormes**	tu	dormis
il	**dorme**	il	dormit
nous	**dormions**	nous	dormîmes
vous	**dormiez**	vous	dormîtes
ils	**dorment**	ils	dormirent

écrire *to write*   Auxiliary: **avoir**

PAST PARTICIPLE	IMPERATIVE
écrit	écris
	écrivons
PRESENT PARTICIPLE	**écrivez**
écrivant	

PRESENT		IMPERFECT	
	j'écris		**j'écrivais**
tu	écris	**tu**	**écrivais**
il	écrit	**il**	**écrivait**
nous	**écrivons**	**nous**	**écrivions**
vous	**écrivez**	**vous**	**écriviez**
ils	**écrivent**	**ils**	**écrivaient**

FUTURE		CONDITIONAL	
	j'écrirai		j'écrirais
tu	écriras	tu	écrirais
il	écrira	il	écrirait
nous	écrirons	nous	écririons
vous	écrirez	vous	écririez
ils	écriront	ils	écriraient

PRESENT SUBJUNCTIVE		PAST HISTORIC	
	j'écrive		**j'écrivis**
tu	**écrives**	tu	**écrivis**
il	**écrive**	il	**écrivit**
nous	**écrivions**	**nous**	**écrivîmes**
vous	**écriviez**	**vous**	**écrivîtes**
ils	**écrivent**	**ils**	**écrivirent**

envoyer *to send*   Auxiliary: **avoir**

PAST PARTICIPLE
envoyé

PRESENT PARTICIPLE
envoyant

IMPERATIVE
envoie
envoyons
envoyez

PRESENT
    j'envoie
  tu envoies
  il envoie
nous envoyons
vous envoyez
ils envoient

IMPERFECT
    j'envoyais
  tu envoyais
  il envoyait
nous envoyions
vous envoyiez
ils envoyaient

FUTURE
    j'enverrai
  tu enverras
  il enverra
nous enverrons
vous enverrez
ils enverront

CONDITIONAL
    j'enverrais
  tu enverrais
  il enverrait
nous enverrions
vous enverriez
ils enverraient

PRESENT SUBJUNCTIVE
    j'envoie
  tu envoies
  il envoie
nous envoyions
vous envoyiez
ils envoient

PAST HISTORIC
    j'envoyai
  tu envoyas
  il envoya
nous envoyâmes
vous envoyâtes
ils envoyèrent

être *to be*   Auxiliary: **avoir**

PAST PARTICIPLE
été

IMPERATIVE
sois
soyons
soyez

PRESENT PARTICIPLE
étant

PRESENT
je	**suis**
tu	**es**
il	**est**
nous	**sommes**
vous	**êtes**
ils	**sont**

IMPERFECT
j'	**étais**
tu	**étais**
il	**était**
nous	**étions**
vous	**étiez**
ils	**étaient**

FUTURE
je	**serai**
tu	**seras**
il	**sera**
nous	**serons**
vous	**serez**
ils	**seront**

CONDITIONAL
je	**serais**
tu	**serais**
il	**serait**
nous	**serions**
vous	**seriez**
ils	**seraient**

PRESENT SUBJUNCTIVE
je	**sois**
tu	**sois**
il	**soit**
nous	**soyons**
vous	**soyez**
ils	**soient**

PAST HISTORIC
je	**fus**
tu	**fus**
il	**fut**
nous	**fûmes**
vous	**fûtes**
ils	**furent**

faire *to do; to make* Auxiliary: **avoir**

PAST PARTICIPLE
fait

PRESENT PARTICIPLE
faisant

IMPERATIVE
fais
faisons
faites

PRESENT		*IMPERFECT*	
je	fais	je	**faisais**
tu	fais	tu	**faisais**
il	fait	il	**faisait**
nous	faisons	nous	**faisions**
vous	faites	vous	**faisiez**
ils	font	ils	**faisaient**

FUTURE		*CONDITIONAL*	
je	ferai	je	**ferais**
tu	feras	tu	**ferais**
il	fera	il	**ferait**
nous	ferons	nous	**ferions**
vous	ferez	vous	**feriez**
ils	feront	ils	**feraient**

PRESENT SUBJUNCTIVE		*PAST HISTORIC*	
je	**fasse**	je	**fis**
tu	**fasses**	tu	**fis**
il	**fasse**	il	**fit**
nous	**fassions**	nous	**fîmes**
vous	**fassiez**	vous	**fîtes**
ils	**fassent**	ils	**firent**

falloir *to be necessary*   Auxiliary: **avoir**

PAST PARTICIPLE
fallu

IMPERATIVE
not used

PRESENT PARTICIPLE
not used

PRESENT	*IMPERFECT*
il faut	**il fallait**

FUTURE	*CONDITIONAL*
il faudra	**il faudrait**

PRESENT SUBJUNCTIVE	*PAST HISTORIC*
il faille	**il fallut**

fuir to flee   Auxiliary: **avoir**

PAST PARTICIPLE
  fui

IMPERATIVE
  fuis
  fuyons
  fuyez

PRESENT PARTICIPLE
  fuyant

PRESENT		IMPERFECT	
je	fuis	**je**	**fuyais**
tu	fuis	**tu**	**fuyais**
il	fuit	**il**	**fuyait**
nous	**fuyons**	**nous**	**fuyions**
vous	**fuyez**	**vous**	**fuyiez**
ils	**fuient**	**ils**	**fuyaient**

FUTURE		CONDITIONAL	
je	fuirai	je	fuirais
tu	fuiras	tu	fuirais
il	fuira	il	fuirait
nous	fuirons	nous	fuirions
vous	fuirez	vous	fuiriez
ils	fuiront	ils	fuiraient

PRESENT SUBJUNCTIVE		PAST HISTORIC	
je	**fuie**	je	fuis
tu	**fuies**	tu	fuis
il	**fuie**	il	fuit
nous	**fuyions**	nous	fuîmes
vous	**fuyiez**	vous	fuîtes
ils	**fuient**	ils	fuirent

haïr *to hate*   Auxiliary: **avoir**

PAST PARTICIPLE **haï**	*IMPERATIVE* hais **haïssons** **haïssez**
PRESENT PARTICIPLE **haïssant**	

PRESENT	*IMPERFECT*
je hais	je **haïssais**
tu hais	tu **haïssais**
il hait	il **haïssait**
nous haïssons	**nous haïssions**
vous haïssez	**vous haïssiez**
ils haïssent	**ils haïssaient**

FUTURE	*CONDITIONAL*
je haïrai	je haïrais
tu haïras	tu haïrais
il haïra	il haïrait
nous haïrons	nous haïrions
vous haïrez	vous haïriez
ils haïront	ils haïraient

PRESENT SUBJUNCTIVE	*PAST HISTORIC*
je haïsse	**je hais**
tu haïsses	**tu hais**
il haïsse	**il hait**
nous haïssions	**nous haïmes**
vous haïssiez	**vous haïtes**
ils haïssent	**ils haïrent**

lire *to read*   Auxiliary: **avoir**

PAST PARTICIPLE **lu**	*IMPERATIVE* **lis** **lisons** **lisez**
PRESENT PARTICIPLE **lisant**	

PRESENT		*IMPERFECT*	
je	lis	je	lisais
tu	lis	tu	lisais
il	lit	il	lisait
nous	lisons	nous	lisions
vous	lisez	vous	lisiez
ils	lisent	ils	lisaient

FUTURE		*CONDITIONAL*	
je	lirai	je	lirais
tu	liras	tu	lirais
il	lira	il	lirait
nous	lirons	nous	lirions
vous	lirez	vous	liriez
ils	liront	ils	liraient

PRESENT SUBJUNCTIVE		*PAST HISTORIC*	
je	lise	je	lus
tu	lises	tu	lus
il	lise	il	lut
nous	lisions	nous	lûmes
vous	lisiez	vous	lûtes
ils	lisent	ils	lurent

mettre *to put*   Auxiliary: **avoir**

PAST PARTICIPLE
mis

PRESENT PARTICIPLE
mettant

IMPERATIVE
mets
mettons
mettez

PRESENT		IMPERFECT	
je	**mets**	je	mettais
tu	**mets**	tu	mettais
il	**met**	il	mettait
nous	mettons	nous	mettions
vous	mettez	vous	mettiez
ils	mettent	ils	mettaient

FUTURE		CONDITIONAL	
je	mettrai	je	mettrais
tu	mettras	tu	mettrais
il	mettra	il	mettrait
nous	mettrons	nous	mettrions
vous	mettrez	vous	mettriez
ils	mettront	ils	mettraient

PRESENT SUBJUNCTIVE		PAST HISTORIC	
je	mette	**je**	**mis**
tu	mettes	**tu**	**mis**
il	mette	**il**	**mit**
nous	mettions	**nous**	**mîmes**
vous	mettiez	**vous**	**mîtes**
ils	mettent	**ils**	**mirent**

moudre to grind   Auxiliary: **avoir**

PAST PARTICIPLE
  moulu

PRESENT PARTICIPLE
  moulant

IMPERATIVE
  mouds
  moulons
  moulez

PRESENT		IMPERFECT	
je	mouds	**je**	**moulais**
tu	mouds	**tu**	**moulais**
il	moud	**il**	**moulait**
nous	**moulons**	**nous**	**moulions**
vous	**moulez**	**vous**	**mouliez**
ils	**moulent**	**ils**	**moulaient**

FUTURE		CONDITIONAL	
je	moudrai	je	moudrais
tu	moudras	tu	moudrais
il	moudra	il	moudrait
nous	moudrons	nous	moudrions
vous	moudrez	vous	moudriez
ils	moudront	ils	moudraient

PRESENT SUBJUNCTIVE		PAST HISTORIC	
je	**moule**	**je**	**moulus**
tu	**moules**	**tu**	**moulus**
il	**moule**	**il**	**moulut**
nous	**moulions**	**nous**	**moulûmes**
vous	**mouliez**	**vous**	**moulûtes**
ils	**moulent**	**ils**	**moulurent**

mourir *to die*   Auxiliary: **être**

PAST PARTICIPLE
mort

IMPERATIVE
meurs
mourons
mourez

PRESENT PARTICIPLE
mourant

PRESENT
je	**meurs**
tu	**meurs**
il	**meurt**
nous	**mourons**
vous	**mourez**
ils	**meurent**

IMPERFECT
je	**mourais**
tu	**mourais**
il	**mourait**
nous	**mourions**
vous	**mouriez**
ils	**mouraient**

FUTURE
je	**mourrai**
tu	**mourras**
il	**mourra**
nous	**mourrons**
vous	**mourrez**
ils	**mourront**

CONDITIONAL
je	**mourrais**
tu	**mourrais**
il	**mourrait**
nous	**mourrions**
vous	**mourriez**
ils	**mourraient**

PRESENT SUBJUNCTIVE
je	**meure**
tu	**meures**
il	**meure**
nous	**mourions**
vous	**mouriez**
ils	**meurent**

PAST HISTORIC
je	**mourus**
tu	**mourus**
il	**mourut**
nous	**mourûmes**
vous	**mourûtes**
ils	**moururent**

naître *to be born*   Auxiliary: **être**

PAST PARTICIPLE	IMPERATIVE
né	**nais**
	naissons
PRESENT PARTICIPLE	**naissez**
naissant	

PRESENT		IMPERFECT	
je	**nais**	**je**	**naissais**
tu	**nais**	**tu**	**naissais**
il	**naît**	**il**	**naissait**
nous	**naissons**	**nous**	**naissions**
vous	**naissez**	**vous**	**naissiez**
ils	**naissent**	**ils**	**naissaient**

FUTURE		CONDITIONAL	
je	naîtrai	je	naîtrais
tu	naîtras	tu	naîtrais
il	naîtra	il	naîtrait
nous	naîtrons	nous	naîtrions
vous	naîtrez	vous	naîtriez
ils	naîtront	ils	naîtraient

PRESENT SUBJUNCTIVE		PAST HISTORIC	
je	**naisse**	je	naquis
tu	**naisses**	tu	naquis
il	**naisse**	il	naquit
nous	**naissions**	nous	naquîmes
vous	**naissiez**	vous	naquîtes
ils	**naissent**	ils	naquirent

ouvrir *to open*   Auxiliary: **avoir**

PAST PARTICIPLE **ouvert**	*IMPERATIVE* **ouvre** **ouvrons** **ouvrez**
PRESENT PARTICIPLE **ouvrant**	

PRESENT	*IMPERFECT*
j'ouvre	**j'ouvrais**
tu ouvres	**tu ouvrais**
il ouvre	**il ouvrait**
nous ouvrons	**nous ouvrions**
vous ouvrez	**vous ouvriez**
ils ouvrent	**ils ouvraient**

FUTURE	*CONDITIONAL*
j'ouvrirai	j'ouvrirais
tu ouvriras	tu ouvrirais
il ouvrira	il ouvrirait
nous ouvrirons	nous ouvririons
vous ouvrirez	vous ouvririez
ils ouvriront	ils ouvriraient

PRESENT SUBJUNCTIVE	*PAST HISTORIC*
j'ouvre	j'ouvris
tu ouvres	tu ouvris
il ouvre	il ouvrit
nous ouvrions	nous ouvrîmes
vous ouvriez	vous ouvrîtes
ils ouvrent	ils ouvrirent

offrir *to offer*, **souffrir** *to suffer* are conjugated similarly

paraître *to appear*   Auxiliary: **avoir**

PAST PARTICIPLE
paru

PRESENT PARTICIPLE
paraissant

IMPERATIVE
parais
paraissons
paraissez

PRESENT
je	**parais**
tu	**parais**
il	**paraît**
nous	**paraissons**
vous	**paraissez**
ils	**paraissent**

IMPERFECT
je	**paraissais**
tu	**paraissais**
il	**paraissait**
nous	**paraissions**
vous	**paraissiez**
ils	**paraissaient**

FUTURE
je	paraîtrai
tu	paraîtras
il	paraîtra
nous	paraîtrons
vous	paraîtrez
ils	paraîtront

CONDITIONAL
je	paraîtrais
tu	paraîtrais
il	paraîtrait
nous	paraîtrions
vous	paraîtriez
ils	paraîtraient

PRESENT SUBJUNCTIVE
je	**paraisse**
tu	**paraisses**
il	**paraisse**
nous	**paraissions**
vous	**paraissiez**
ils	**paraissent**

PAST HISTORIC
je	**parus**
tu	**parus**
il	**parut**
nous	**parûmes**
vous	**parûtes**
ils	**parurent**

partir to leave   Auxiliary: **être**

PAST PARTICIPLE parti	*IMPERATIVE* **pars** **partons** **partez**
PRESENT PARTICIPLE **partant**	

PRESENT		*IMPERFECT*	
je	**pars**	je	**partais**
tu	**pars**	tu	**partais**
il	**part**	il	**partait**
nous	**partons**	nous	**partions**
vous	**partez**	vous	**partiez**
ils	**partent**	ils	**partaient**

FUTURE		*CONDITIONAL*	
je	partirai	je	partirais
tu	partiras	tu	partirais
il	partira	il	partirait
nous	partirons	nous	partirions
vous	partirez	vous	partiriez
ils	partiront	ils	partiraient

PRESENT SUBJUNCTIVE		*PAST HISTORIC*	
je	**parte**	je	partis
tu	**partes**	tu	partis
il	**parte**	il	partit
nous	**partions**	nous	partîmes
vous	**partiez**	vous	partîtes
ils	**partent**	ils	partirent

plaire to please   Auxiliary: **avoir**

PAST PARTICIPLE
  plu

IMPERATIVE
  plais
  plaisons
  plaisez

PRESENT PARTICIPLE
  plaisant

PRESENT
  je   plais
  tu   plais
  il   **plaît**
  nous plaisons
  vous plaisez
  ils plaisent

IMPERFECT
  je   **plaisais**
  tu   **plaisais**
  il   **plaisait**
  nous **plaisions**
  vous **plaisiez**
  ils **plaisaient**

FUTURE
  je   plairai
  tu   plairas
  il   plaira
  nous plairons
  vous plairez
  ils plairont

CONDITIONAL
  je   plairais
  tu   plairais
  il   plairait
  nous plairions
  vous plairiez
  ils plairaient

PRESENT SUBJUNCTIVE
  je   **plaise**
  tu   **plaises**
  il   **plaise**
  nous plaisions
  vous plaisiez
  ils plaisent

PAST HISTORIC
  je   **plus**
  tu   **plus**
  il   **plut**
  nous **plûmes**
  vous **plûtes**
  ils **plurent**

pleuvoir *to rain*   Auxiliary: **avoir**

PAST PARTICIPLE
plu

IMPERATIVE
not used

PRESENT PARTICIPLE
pleuvant

PRESENT
  il **pleut**

IMPERFECT
  il **pleuvait**

FUTURE
  il **pleuvra**

CONDITIONAL
  il **pleuvrait**

PRESENT SUBJUNCTIVE
  il **pleuve**

PAST HISTORIC
  il **plut**

pouvoir *to be able to*　　　　Auxiliary: **avoir**

PAST PARTICIPLE
pu

IMPERATIVE
not used

PRESENT PARTICIPLE
pouvant

PRESENT		*IMPERFECT*	
je	peux*	je	pouvais
tu	peux	tu	pouvais
il	peut	il	pouvait
nous	pouvons	nous	pouvions
vous	pouvez	vous	pouviez
ils	peuvent	ils	pouvaient

FUTURE		*CONDITIONAL*	
je	pourrai	je	pourrais
tu	pourras	tu	pourrais
il	pourra	il	pourrait
nous	pourrons	nous	pourrions
vous	pourrez	vous	pourriez
ils	pourront	ils	pourraient

PRESENT SUBJUNCTIVE		*PAST HISTORIC*	
je	puisse	je	pus
tu	puisses	tu	pus
il	puisse	il	put
nous	puissions	nous	pûmes
vous	puissiez	vous	pûtes
ils	puissent	ils	purent

*In questions: **puis-je?**

prendre *to take*

Auxiliary: **avoir**

PAST PARTICIPLE
pris

PRESENT PARTICIPLE
prenant

IMPERATIVE
prends
prenons
prenez

PRESENT

je	prends
tu	prends
il	prend
nous	**prenons**
vous	**prenez**
ils	**prennent**

IMPERFECT

je	**prenais**
tu	**prenais**
il	**prenait**
nous	prenions
vous	preniez
ils	**prenaient**

FUTURE

je	prendrai
tu	prendras
il	prendra
nous	prendrons
vous	prendrez
ils	prendront

CONDITIONAL

je	prendrais
tu	prendrais
il	prendrait
nous	prendrions
vous	prendriez
ils	prendraient

PRESENT SUBJUNCTIVE

je	**prenne**
tu	**prennes**
il	**prenne**
nous	**prenions**
vous	**preniez**
ils	**prennent**

PAST HISTORIC

je	**pris**
tu	**pris**
il	**prit**
nous	**prîmes**
vous	**prîtes**
ils	**prirent**

recevoir to receive   Auxiliary: avoir

PAST PARTICIPLE
reçu

IMPERATIVE
reçois
recevons
recevez

PRESENT PARTICIPLE
recevant

PRESENT		IMPERFECT	
je	reçois	je	recevais
tu	reçois	tu	recevais
il	reçoit	il	recevait
nous	recevons	nous	recevions
vous	recevez	vous	receviez
ils	reçoivent	ils	recevaient

FUTURE		CONDITIONAL	
je	recevrai	je	recevrais
tu	recevras	tu	recevrais
il	recevra	il	recevrait
nous	recevrons	nous	recevrions
vous	recevrez	vous	recevriez
ils	recevront	ils	recevraient

PRESENT SUBJUNCTIVE		PAST HISTORIC	
je	reçoive	je	reçus
tu	reçoives	tu	reçus
il	reçoive	il	reçut
nous	recevions	nous	reçûmes
vous	receviez	vous	reçûtes
ils	reçoivent	ils	reçurent

résoudre *to solve*   Auxiliary: **avoir**

PAST PARTICIPLE
résolu

IMPERATIVE
résous
résolvons
résolvez

PRESENT PARTICIPLE
résolvant

	PRESENT		*IMPERFECT*
je	**résous**	je	**résolvais**
tu	**résous**	tu	**résolvais**
il	**résout**	il	**résolvait**
nous	**résolvons**	nous	**résolvions**
vous	**résolvez**	vous	**résolviez**
ils	**résolvent**	ils	**résolvaient**

	FUTURE		*CONDITIONAL*
je	résoudrai	je	résoudrais
tu	résoudras	tu	résoudrais
il	résoudra	il	résoudrait
nous	résoudrons	nous	résoudrions
vous	résoudrez	vous	résoudriez
ils	résoudront	ils	résoudraient

	PRESENT SUBJUNCTIVE		*PAST HISTORIC*
je	**résolve**	je	**résolus**
tu	**résolves**	tu	**résolus**
il	**résolve**	il	**résolut**
nous	**résolvions**	nous	**résolûmes**
vous	**résolviez**	vous	**résolûtes**
ils	**résolvent**	ils	**résolurent**

rire to laugh   Auxiliary: **avoir**

PAST PARTICIPLE
  ri

PRESENT PARTICIPLE
  riant

IMPERATIVE
ris
rions
riez

PRESENT		*IMPERFECT*	
je	ris	je	riais
tu	ris	tu	riais
il	**rit**	il	riait
nous	rions	nous	riions
vous	riez	vous	riiez
ils	rient	ils	riaient

FUTURE		*CONDITIONAL*	
je	rirai	je	rirais
tu	riras	tu	rirais
il	rira	il	rirait
nous	rirons	nous	ririons
vous	rirez	vous	ririez
ils	riront	ils	riraient

PRESENT SUBJUNCTIVE		*PAST HISTORIC*	
je	rie	**je**	**ris**
tu	ries	**tu**	**ris**
il	rie	**il**	**rit**
nous	riions	**nous**	**rîmes**
vous	riiez	**vous**	**rîtes**
ils	rient	**ils**	**rirent**

rompre to break   Auxiliary: **avoir**

PAST PARTICIPLE
rompu

IMPERATIVE
romps
rompons
rompez

PRESENT PARTICIPLE
rompant

PRESENT
je	romps
tu	romps
il	**rompt**
nous	rompons
vous	rompez
ils	rompent

IMPERFECT
je	rompais
tu	rompais
il	rompait
nous	rompions
vous	rompiez
ils	rompaient

FUTURE
je	romprai
tu	rompras
il	rompra
nous	romprons
vous	romprez
ils	rompront

CONDITIONAL
je	romprais
tu	romprais
il	romprait
nous	romprions
vous	rompriez
ils	rompraient

PRESENT SUBJUNCTIVE
je	rompe
tu	rompes
il	rompe
nous	rompions
vous	rompiez
ils	rompent

PAST HISTORIC
je	rompis
tu	rompis
il	rompit
nous	rompîmes
vous	rompîtes
ils	rompirent

savoir to know   Auxiliary: **avoir**

PAST PARTICIPLE
  su

IMPERATIVE
  sache
  sachons
  sachez

PRESENT PARTICIPLE
  sachant

PRESENT		IMPERFECT	
je	**sais**	je	**savais**
tu	**sais**	tu	**savais**
il	**sait**	il	**savait**
nous	**savons**	nous	**savions**
vous	**savez**	vous	**saviez**
ils	**savent**	ils	**savaient**

FUTURE		CONDITIONAL	
je	**saurai**	je	**saurais**
tu	**sauras**	tu	**saurais**
il	**saura**	il	**saurait**
nous	**saurons**	nous	**saurions**
vous	**saurez**	vous	**sauriez**
ils	**sauront**	ils	**sauraient**

PRESENT SUBJUNCTIVE		PAST HISTORIC	
je	**sache**	je	**sus**
tu	**saches**	tu	**sus**
il	**sache**	il	**sut**
nous	**sachions**	nous	**sûmes**
vous	**sachiez**	vous	**sûtes**
ils	**sachent**	ils	**surent**

sentir *to feel; to smell*　　　　Auxiliary: **avoir**

PAST PARTICIPLE	IMPERATIVE
senti	**sens**
	sentons
PRESENT PARTICIPLE	**sentez**
sentant	

PRESENT		IMPERFECT	
je	**sens**	**je**	**sentais**
tu	**sens**	**tu**	**sentais**
il	**sent**	**il**	**sentait**
nous	**sentons**	**nous**	**sentions**
vous	**sentez**	**vous**	**sentiez**
ils	**sentent**	**ils**	**sentaient**

FUTURE		CONDITIONAL	
je	sentirai	je	sentirais
tu	sentiras	tu	sentirais
il	sentira	il	sentirait
nous	sentirons	nous	sentirions
vous	sentirez	vous	sentiriez
ils	sentiront	ils	sentiraient

PRESENT SUBJUNCTIVE		PAST HISTORIC	
je	**sente**	je	sentis
tu	**sentes**	tu	sentis
il	**sente**	il	sentit
nous	**sentions**	nous	sentîmes
vous	**sentiez**	vous	sentîtes
ils	**sentent**	ils	sentirent

servir to serve   Auxiliary: **avoir**

PAST PARTICIPLE
  servi

IMPERATIVE
  sers
  servons
  servez

PRESENT PARTICIPLE
  servant

PRESENT
je	**sers**
tu	**sers**
il	**sert**
nous	**servons**
vous	**servez**
ils	**servent**

IMPERFECT
je	**servais**
tu	**servais**
il	**servait**
nous	**servions**
vous	**serviez**
ils	**servaient**

FUTURE
je	servirai
tu	serviras
il	servira
nous	servirons
vous	servirez
ils	serviront

CONDITIONAL
je	servirais
tu	servirais
il	servirait
nous	servirions
vous	serviriez
ils	serviraient

PRESENT SUBJUNCTIVE
je	**serve**
tu	**serves**
il	**serve**
nous	**servions**
vous	**serviez**
ils	**servent**

PAST HISTORIC
je	servis
tu	servis
il	servit
nous	servîmes
vous	servîtes
ils	servirent

sortir *to go/come out*   Auxiliary: **être**

PAST PARTICIPLE
sorti

IMPERATIVE
sors
sortons
sortez

PRESENT PARTICIPLE
sortant

PRESENT
je	**sors**
tu	**sors**
il	**sort**
nous	**sortons**
vous	**sortez**
ils	**sortent**

IMPERFECT
je	**sortais**
tu	**sortais**
il	**sortait**
nous	**sortions**
vous	**sortiez**
ils	**sortaient**

FUTURE
je	sortirai
tu	sortiras
il	sortira
nous	sortirons
vous	sortirez
ils	sortiront

CONDITIONAL
je	sortirais
tu	sortirais
il	sortirait
nous	sortirions
vous	sortiriez
ils	sortiraient

PRESENT SUBJUNCTIVE
je	**sorte**
tu	**sortes**
il	**sorte**
nous	**sortions**
vous	**sortiez**
ils	**sortent**

PAST HISTORIC
je	sortis
tu	sortis
il	sortit
nous	sortîmes
vous	sortîtes
ils	sortirent

suffire *to be enough* Auxiliary: **avoir**

PAST PARTICIPLE
suffi

IMPERATIVE
suffis
suffisons
suffisez

PRESENT PARTICIPLE
suffisant

PRESENT		IMPERFECT	
je	suffis	je	**suffisais**
tu	suffis	tu	**suffisais**
il	suffit	il	**suffisait**
nous	**suffisons**	**nous**	**suffisions**
vous	**suffisez**	**vous**	**suffisiez**
ils	**suffisent**	**ils**	**suffisaient**

FUTURE		CONDITIONAL	
je	suffirai	je	suffirais
tu	suffiras	tu	suffirais
il	suffira	il	suffirait
nous	suffirons	nous	suffirions
vous	suffirez	vous	suffiriez
ils	suffiront	ils	suffiraient

PRESENT SUBJUNCTIVE		PAST HISTORIC	
je	**suffise**	**je**	**suffis**
tu	**suffises**	**tu**	**suffis**
il	**suffise**	**il**	**suffit**
nous	**suffisions**	**nous**	**suffîmes**
vous	**suffisiez**	**vous**	**suffîtes**
ils	**suffisent**	**ils**	**suffirent**

suivre to follow   Auxiliary: **avoir**

PAST PARTICIPLE
suivi

IMPERATIVE
suis
suivons
suivez

PRESENT PARTICIPLE
suivant

PRESENT		IMPERFECT	
je	**suis**	je	suivais
tu	**suis**	tu	suivais
il	**suit**	il	suivait
nous	suivons	nous	suivions
vous	suivez	vous	suiviez
ils	suivent	ils	suivaient

FUTURE		CONDITIONAL	
je	suivrai	je	suivrais
tu	suivras	tu	suivrais
il	suivra	il	suivrait
nous	suivrons	nous	suivrions
vous	suivrez	vous	suivriez
ils	suivront	ils	suivraient

PRESENT SUBJUNCTIVE		PAST HISTORIC	
je	suive	je	suivis
tu	suives	tu	suivis
il	suive	il	suivit
nous	suivions	nous	suivîmes
vous	suiviez	vous	suivîtes
ils	suivent	ils	suivirent

se taire to stop talking   Auxiliary: **être**

PAST PARTICIPLE
tu

PRESENT PARTICIPLE
se taisant

IMPERATIVE
tais-toi
taisons-nous
taisez-vous

PRESENT		*IMPERFECT*	
je	me tais	je	me taisais
tu	te tais	tu	te taisais
il	se tait	il	se taisait
nous	**nous taisons**	**nous**	**nous taisions**
vous	**vous taisez**	**vous**	**vous taisiez**
ils	**se taisent**	**ils**	**se taisaient**

FUTURE		*CONDITIONAL*	
je	me tairai	je	me tairais
tu	te tairas	tu	te tairais
il	se taira	il	se tairait
nous	nous tairons	nous	nous tairions
vous	vous tairez	vous	vous tairiez
ils	se tairont	ils	se tairaient

PRESENT SUBJUNCTIVE		*PAST HISTORIC*	
je	**me taise**	**je**	**me tus**
tu	**te taises**	**tu**	**te tus**
il	**se taise**	**il**	**se tut**
nous	**nous taisions**	**nous**	**nous tûmes**
vous	**vous taisiez**	**vous**	**vous tûtes**
ils	**se taisent**	**ils**	**se turent**

tenir *to hold*   Auxiliary: **avoir**

PAST PARTICIPLE
tenu

PRESENT PARTICIPLE
tenant

IMPERATIVE
tiens
tenons
tenez

PRESENT		*IMPERFECT*	
je	tiens	je	tenais
tu	tiens	tu	tenais
il	tient	il	tenait
nous	tenons	nous	tenions
vous	tenez	vous	teniez
ils	tiennent	ils	tenaient

FUTURE		*CONDITIONAL*	
je	tiendrai	je	tiendrais
tu	tiendras	tu	tiendrais
il	tiendra	il	tiendrait
nous	tiendrons	nous	tiendrions
vous	tiendrez	vous	tiendriez
ils	tiendront	ils	tiendraient

PRESENT SUBJUNCTIVE		*PAST HISTORIC*	
je	tienne	je	tins
tu	tiennes	tu	tins
il	tienne	il	tint
nous	tenions	nous	tînmes
vous	teniez	vous	tîntes
ils	tiennent	ils	tinrent

vaincre to defeat

Auxiliary: **avoir**

PAST PARTICIPLE
vaincu

PRESENT PARTICIPLE
vainquant

IMPERATIVE
vaincs
vainquons
vainquez

PRESENT		IMPERFECT	
je	vaincs	je	**vainquais**
tu	vaincs	tu	**vainquais**
il	vainc	il	**vainquait**
nous	**vainquons**	**nous**	**vainquions**
vous	**vainquez**	**vous**	**vainquiez**
ils	**vainquent**	**ils**	**vainquaient**

FUTURE		CONDITIONAL	
je	vaincrai	je	vaincrais
tu	vaincras	tu	vaincrais
il	vaincra	il	vaincrait
nous	vaincrons	nous	vaincrions
vous	vaincrez	vous	vaincriez
ils	vaincront	ils	vaincraient

PRESENT SUBJUNCTIVE		PAST HISTORIC	
je	**vainque**	**je**	**vainquis**
tu	**vainques**	**tu**	**vainquis**
il	**vainque**	**il**	**vainquit**
nous	**vainquions**	**nous**	**vainquîmes**
vous	**vainquiez**	**vous**	**vainquîtes**
ils	**vainquent**	**ils**	**vainquirent**

valoir to be worth
Auxiliary: **avoir**

PAST PARTICIPLE
valu

IMPERATIVE
vaux
valons
valez

PRESENT PARTICIPLE
valant

PRESENT		IMPERFECT	
je	vaux	je	valais
tu	vaux	tu	valais
il	vaut	il	valait
nous	valons	nous	valions
vous	valez	vous	valiez
ils	valent	ils	valaient

FUTURE		CONDITIONAL	
je	vaudrai	je	vaudrais
tu	vaudras	tu	vaudrais
il	vaudra	il	vaudrait
nous	vaudrons	nous	vaudrions
vous	vaudrez	vous	vaudriez
ils	vaudront	ils	vaudraient

PRESENT SUBJUNCTIVE		PAST HISTORIC	
je	vaille	je	valus
tu	vailles	tu	valus
il	vaille	il	valut
nous	valions	nous	valûmes
vous	valiez	vous	valûtes
ils	vaillent	ils	valurent

venir *to come*   Auxiliary: **être**

PAST PARTICIPLE
venu

PRESENT PARTICIPLE
venant

IMPERATIVE
viens
venons
venez

PRESENT		*IMPERFECT*	
je	viens	je	venais
tu	viens	tu	venais
il	vient	il	venait
nous	venons	nous	venions
vous	venez	vous	veniez
ils	viennent	ils	venaient

FUTURE		*CONDITIONAL*	
je	viendrai	je	viendrais
tu	viendras	tu	viendrais
il	viendra	il	viendrait
nous	viendrons	nous	viendrions
vous	viendrez	vous	viendriez
ils	viendront	ils	viendraient

PRESENT SUBJUNCTIVE		*PAST HISTORIC*	
je	vienne	je	vins
tu	viennes	tu	vins
il	vienne	il	vint
nous	venions	nous	vînmes
vous	veniez	vous	vîntes
ils	viennent	ils	vinrent

vêtir *to dress*   Auxiliary: **avoir**

PAST PARTICIPLE
vêtu

PRESENT PARTICIPLE
vêtant

IMPERATIVE
vêts
vêtons
vêtez

PRESENT		IMPERFECT	
je	**vêts**	je	**vêtais**
tu	**vêts**	tu	**vêtais**
il	**vêt**	il	**vêtait**
nous	**vêtons**	nous	**vêtions**
vous	**vêtez**	vous	**vêtiez**
ils	**vêtent**	ils	**vêtaient**

FUTURE		CONDITIONAL	
je	vêtirai	je	vêtirais
tu	vêtiras	tu	vêtirais
il	vêtira	il	vêtirait
nous	vêtirons	nous	vêtirions
vous	vêtirez	vous	vêtiriez
ils	vêtiront	ils	vêtiraient

PRESENT SUBJUNCTIVE		PAST HISTORIC	
je	**vête**	je	vêtis
tu	**vêtes**	tu	vêtis
il	**vête**	il	vêtit
nous	**vêtions**	nous	vêtîmes
vous	**vêtiez**	vous	vêtîtes
ils	**vêtent**	ils	vêtirent

vivre *to live*   Auxiliary: **avoir**

PAST PARTICIPLE
vécu

PRESENT PARTICIPLE
vivant

IMPERATIVE
vis
vivons
vivez

PRESENT		*IMPERFECT*	
je	**vis**	je	vivais
tu	**vis**	tu	vivais
il	**vit**	il	vivait
nous	vivons	nous	vivions
vous	vivez	vous	viviez
ils	vivent	ils	vivaient

FUTURE		*CONDITIONAL*	
je	vivrai	je	vivrais
tu	vivras	tu	vivrais
il	vivra	il	vivrait
nous	vivrons	nous	vivrions
vous	vivrez	vous	vivriez
ils	vivront	ils	vivraient

PRESENT SUBJUNCTIVE		*PAST HISTORIC*	
je	vive	**je**	**vécus**
tu	vives	**tu**	**vécus**
il	vive	**il**	**vécut**
nous	vivions	**nous**	**vécûmes**
vous	viviez	**vous**	**vécûtes**
ils	vivent	**ils**	**vécurent**

voir *to see*   Auxiliary: **avoir**

PAST PARTICIPLE
  vu

IMPERATIVE
  vois
  voyons
  voyez

PRESENT PARTICIPLE
  voyant

PRESENT		IMPERFECT	
je	vois	je	voyais
tu	vois	tu	voyais
il	voit	il	voyait
nous	voyons	nous	voyions
vous	voyez	vous	voyiez
ils	voient	ils	voyaient

FUTURE		CONDITIONAL	
je	verrai	je	verrais
tu	verras	tu	verrais
il	verra	il	verrait
nous	verrons	nous	verrions
vous	verrez	vous	verriez
ils	verront	ils	verraient

PRESENT SUBJUNCTIVE		PAST HISTORIC	
je	voie	je	vis
tu	voies	tu	vis
il	voie	il	vit
nous	voyions	nous	vîmes
vous	voyiez	vous	vîtes
ils	voient	ils	virent

vouloir *to wish, want*   Auxiliary: **avoir**

PAST PARTICIPLE	IMPERATIVE
voulu	**veuille**
	veuillons
PRESENT PARTICIPLE	**veuillez**
voulant	

PRESENT		IMPERFECT	
je	veux	je	voulais
tu	veux	tu	voulais
il	veut	il	voulait
nous	voulons	nous	voulions
vous	voulez	vous	vouliez
ils	veulent	ils	voulaient

FUTURE		CONDITIONAL	
je	voudrai	je	voudrais
tu	voudras	tu	voudrais
il	voudra	il	voudrait
nous	voudrons	nous	voudrions
vous	voudrez	vous	voudriez
ils	voudront	ils	voudraient

PRESENT SUBJUNCTIVE		PAST HISTORIC	
je	veuille	je	voulus
tu	veuilles	tu	voulus
il	veuille	il	voulut
nous	voulions	nous	voulûmes
vous	vouliez	vous	voulûtes
ils	veuillent	ils	voulurent

The Gender of Nouns

In French, all nouns are either masculine or feminine, whether denoting people, animals or things. Unlike English, there is no neuter gender for inanimate objects and abstract nouns.

Gender is largely unpredictable and has to be learnt for each noun. However, the following guidelines will help you determine the gender for certain types of nouns.

- Nouns denoting male people and animals are usually – but not always – masculine, e.g.

un homme	**un taureau**
a man	*a bull*
un infirmier	**un cheval**
a (male) nurse	*a horse*

- Nouns denoting female people and animals are usually – but not always – feminine, e.g.

une fille	**une vache**
a girl	*a cow*
une infirmière	**une brebis**
a nurse	*a ewe*

- Some nouns are masculine OR feminine depending on the sex of the person to whom they refer, e.g.

un camarade	**une camarade**
a (male) friend	*a (female) friend*
un Belge	**une Belge**
a Belgian (man)	*a Belgian (woman)*

- Other nouns referring to either men or women have only one gender which applies to both, e.g.

un professeur	**une personne**	**une sentinelle**
a teacher	*a person*	*a sentry*
un témoin	**une victime**	**une recrue**
a witness	*a victim*	*a recruit*

● Sometimes the ending of the noun indicates its gender. Shown below are some of the most important to guide you:

Masculine endings

-age	**le courage** *courage*, **le rinçage** *rinsing*
	EXCEPTIONS: **une cage** *a cage*, **une image** *a picture*, **la nage** *swimming*, **une page** *a page*, **une plage** *a beach*, **une rage** *a rage*
-ment	**le commencement** *the beginning*
	EXCEPTION: **une jument** *a mare*
-oir	**un couloir** *a corridor*, **un miroir** *a mirror*
-sme	**le pessimisme** *pessimism*, **l'enthousiasme** *enthusiasm*

Feminine endings

-ance, anse	**la confiance** *confidence*, **la danse** *dancing*
-ence, -ense	**la prudence** *caution*, **la défense** *defence*
	EXCEPTION: **le silence** *silence*
-ion	**une région** *a region*, **une addition** *a bill*
	EXCEPTIONS: **un pion** *a pawn*, **un espion** *a spy*
-oire	**une baignoire** *a bath(tub)*
-té, -tié	**la beauté** *beauty*, **la moitié** *half*

● Suffixes which differentiate between male and female are shown on pp. 134 and 136

● The following words have different meanings depending on gender:

le crêpe	*crêpe*	la crêpe	*pancake*
le livre	*book*	la livre	*pound*
le manche	*handle*	la manche	*sleeve*
le mode	*method*	la mode	*fashion*
le moule	*mould*	la moule	*mussel*
le page	*page(boy)*	la page	*page (in book)*
le physique	*physique*	la physique	*physics*
le poêle	*stove*	la poêle	*frying pan*
le somme	*nap*	la somme	*sum*
le tour	*turn*	la tour	*tower*
le voile	*veil*	la voile	*sail*

Gender: the formation of feminines

As in English, male and female are sometimes differentiated by the use of two quite separate words, e.g.

mon oncle	**ma tante**
my uncle	*my aunt*
un taureau	**une vache**
a bull	*a cow*

There are, however, some words in French which show this distinction by the form of their ending

- Some nouns add an **e** to the masculine singular form to form the feminine (**→ 1**)

- If the masculine singular form already ends in **-e**, no further **e** is added in the feminine (**→ 2**)

- Some nouns undergo a further change when **e** is added. These changes occur regularly and are shown on p. 136

Feminine forms to note

MASCULINE	FEMININE	
un âne	une ânesse	*donkey*
le comte	la comtesse	*count/countess*
le duc	la duchesse	*duke/duchess*
un Esquimau	une Esquimaude	*Eskimo*
le fou	la folle	*madman/madwoman*
le Grec	la Grecque	*Greek*
un hôte	une hôtesse	*host/hostess*
le jumeau	la jumelle	*twin*
le maître	la maîtresse	*master/mistress*
le prince	la princesse	*prince/princess*
le tigre	la tigresse	*tiger/tigress*
le traître	la traîtresse	*traitor*
le Turc	la Turque	*Turk*
le vieux	la vieille	*old man/old woman*

Continued

1 un ami
 a (male) friend
un employé
 a (male) employee
un Français
 a Frenchman

une amie
 a (female) friend
une employée
 a (female) employee
une Française
 a Frenchwoman

2 un élève
 a (male) pupil
un collègue
 a (male) colleague
un camarade
 a (male) friend

une élève
 a (female) pupil
une collègue
 a (female) colleague
une camarade
 a (female) friend

Regular feminine endings

MASC. SING.	FEM. SING.	
-f	-ve	(→ 1)
-x	-se	(→ 2)
-eur	-euse	(→ 3)
-teur	⎧ -teuse	(→ 4)
	⎩ -trice	(→ 5)

Some nouns double the final consonant before adding **e**:

MASC. SING.	FEM. SING.	
-an	-anne	(→ 6)
-en	-enne	(→ 7)
-on	-onne	(→ 8)
-et	-ette	(→ 9)
-el	-elle	(→ 10)

Some nouns add an accent to the final syllable before adding **e**:

MASC. SING.	FEM. SING.	
-er	-ère	(→ 11)

Pronunciation and feminine endings

This is dealt with on p. 244.

1 **un sportif**
a sportsman
un veuf
a widower

    une sportive
a sportswoman
une veuve
a widow

2 **un époux**
a husband
un amoureux
a man in love

    une épouse
a wife
une amoureuse
a woman in love

3 **un danseur**
a dancer
un voleur
a thief

    une danseuse
a dancer
une voleuse
a thief

4 **un menteur**
a liar
un chanteur
a singer

    une menteuse
a liar
une chanteuse
a singer

5 **un acteur**
an actor
un conducteur
a driver

    une actrice
an actress
une conductrice
a driver

6 **un paysan**
a countryman

    une paysanne
a countrywoman

7 **un Parisien**
a Parisian

    une Parisienne
a Parisian (woman)

8 **un baron**
a baron

    une baronne
a baroness

9 **le cadet**
the youngest (child)

    la cadette
the youngest (child)

10 **un intellectuel**
an intellectual

    une intellectuelle
an intellectual

11 **un étranger**
a foreigner
le dernier
the last (one)

    une étrangère
a foreigner
la dernière
the last (one)

The formation of plurals

● Most nouns add **s** to the singular form (→ **1**)

● When the singular form already ends in **-s**, **-x** or **-z**, no further **s** is added (→ **2**)

● For nouns ending in **-au**, **-eau** or **-eu**, the plural ends in **-aux**, **-eaux** or **-eux** (→ **3**)

Exceptions:	**pneu**	*tyre*	(plur: **pneus**)
	bleu	*bruise*	(plur: **bleus**)

● For nouns ending in **-al** or **-ail**, the plural ends in **-aux** (→ **4**)

Exceptions:	**bal**	*ball*	(plur: **bals**)
	festival	*festival*	(plur: **festivals**)
	chandail	*sweater*	(plur: **chandails**)
	détail	*detail*	(plur: **détails**)

● Forming the plural of compound nouns is complicated and you are advised to check each one individually in a dictionary

Irregular plural forms

● Some masculine nouns ending in **-ou** add **x** in the plural. These are:

bijou	*jewel*	**genou**	*knee*	**joujou**	*toy*
caillou	*pebble*	**hibou**	*owl*	**pou**	*louse*
chou	*cabbage*				

● Some other nouns are totally unpredictable. Chief among these are:

SINGULAR	PLURAL
œil *eye*	**yeux**
ciel *sky*	**cieux**
Monsieur *Mr.*	**Messieurs**
Madame *Mrs.*	**Mesdames**
Mademoiselle *Miss*	**Mesdemoiselles**

Pronunciation of plural forms
This is dealt with on p. 244

1 le jardin
the garden
une voiture
a car
l'hôtel
the hotel

les jardins
the gardens
des voitures
(some) cars
les hôtels
the hotels

2 un tas
a heap
une voix
a voice
le gaz
the gas

des tas
(some) heaps
des voix
(some) voices
les gaz
the gases

3 un tuyau
a pipe
le chapeau
the hat
le feu
the fire

des tuyaux
(some) pipes
les chapeaux
the hats
les feux
the fires

4 le journal
the newspaper
un travail
a job

les journaux
the newspapers
des travaux
(some) jobs

The Definite Article

	WITH MASC. NOUN	WITH FEM. NOUN	
SING.	le (l')	la (l')	the
PLUR.	les	les	the

- The gender and number of the noun determines the form of the article (→ **1**)

- **le** and **la** change to **l'** before a vowel or an **h** 'mute' (→ **2**)

- For uses of the definite article see p. 142

- **à + le/la (l'), à + les**

	WITH MASC. NOUN	WITH FEM. NOUN	
SING.	au (à l')	à la (à l')	
PLUR.	aux	aux	(→ **3**)

- The definite article combines with the preposition **à**, as shown above. You should pay particular attention to the masculine singular form **au**, and both plural forms **aux**, since these are not visually the sum of their parts

- **de + le/la (l'), de + les**

	WITH MASC. NOUN	WITH FEM. NOUN	
SING.	du (de l')	de la (de l')	
PLUR.	des	des	(→ **4**)

- The definite article combines with the preposition **de**, as shown above. You should pay particular attention to the masculine singular form **du**, and both plural forms **des**, since these are not visually the sum of their parts

Continued

MASCULINE	FEMININE
1 le train	**la gare**
the train	the station
le garçon	**la fille**
the boy	the girl
les hôtels	**les écoles**
the hotels	the schools
les professeurs	**les femmes**
the teachers	the women
2 l'acteur	**l'actrice**
the actor	the actress
l'effet	**l'eau**
the effect	the water
l'ingrédient	**l'idée**
the ingredient	the idea
l'objet	**l'ombre**
the object	the shadow
l'univers	**l'usine**
the universe	the factory
l'hôpital	**l'heure**
the hospital	the time
3 au cinéma	**à la bibliothèque**
at/to the cinema	at/to the library
à l'employé	**à l'infirmière**
to the employee	to the nurse
à l'hôpital	**à l'hôtesse**
at/to the hospital	to the hostess
aux étudiants	**aux maisons**
to the students	to the houses
4 du bureau	**de la réunion**
from/of the office	from/of the meeting
de l'auteur	**de l'Italienne**
from/of the author	from/of the Italian woman
de l'hôte	**de l'horloge**
from/of the host	of the clock
des Etats-Unis	**des vendeuses**
from/of the United States	from/of the saleswomen

Uses of the definite article

While the definite article is used in much the same way in French as it is in English, its use is more widespread in French. Unlike English the definite article is also used:

- with abstract nouns, except when following certain prepositions (→ **1**)

- in generalisations, especially with plural or uncountable* nouns (→ **2**)

- with names of countries (→ **3**)
  Exceptions: no article with countries following **en** *to/in* (→ **4**)

- with parts of the body (→ **5**)
  'Ownership' is often indicated by an indirect object pronoun or a reflexive pronoun (→ **6**)

- in expressions of quantity/rate/price (→ **7**)

- with titles/ranks/professions followed by a proper name (→ **8**)

- The definite article is NOT used with nouns in apposition (→ **9**)

*An uncountable noun is one which cannot be used in the plural or with an indefinite article, e.g. **l'acier** *steel*, **le lait** *milk*

1 **Les prix montent**
Prices are rising
L'amour rayonne dans ses yeux
Love shines in his eyes
BUT   **avec plaisir**   **sans espoir**
       with pleasure   without hope

2 **Je n'aime pas le café**
I don't like coffee
Les enfants ont besoin d'être aimés
Children need to be loved

3 **le Japon   la France   l'Italie   les Pays-Bas**
Japan   France   Italy   The Netherlands

4 **aller en Ecosse**   **Il travaille en Allemagne**
to go to Scotland   He works in Germany

5 **Tournez la tête à gauche**
Turn your head to the left
J'ai mal à la gorge
My throat is sore, I have a sore throat

6 **La tête me tourne**
My head is spinning
Elle s'est brossé les dents
She brushed her teeth

7 **40 francs le mètre/le kilo/la douzaine/la pièce**
40 francs a metre/a kilo/a dozen/each
rouler à 80 km à l'heure
to go at 50 m.p.h.
payé à l'heure/au jour/au mois
paid by the hour/by the day/by the month

8 **le roi Georges III**   **le capitaine Darbeau**
King George III   Captain Darbeau
le docteur Rousseau   **Monsieur le président**
Dr. Rousseau   Mr. Chairman/President

9 **Victor Hugo, grand écrivain du dix-neuvième siècle**
Victor Hugo, a great author of the nineteenth century
Joseph Leblanc, inventeur et entrepreneur, a été le premier ...
Joseph Leblanc, an inventor and entrepreneur, was the first ...

The Partitive Article

The partitive article has the sense of *some* or *any*, although the French is not always translated in English.

Forms of the partitive

	WITH MASC. NOUN	WITH FEM. NOUN	
SING.	**du (de l')**	**de la (de l')**	some, any
PLUR.	**des**	**des**	some, any

- The gender and number of the noun determines the form of the partitive (→ **1**)

- The forms shown in brackets are used before a vowel or an **h** 'mute' (→ **2**)

- **des** becomes **de** (**d'** + vowel) before an adjective (→ **3**), unless the adjective and noun are seen as forming one unit (→ **4**)

- In negative sentences **de** (**d'** + vowel) is used for both genders, singular and plural (→ **5**)
  Exception: after **ne ... que** *only*, the positive forms above are used (→ **6**)

1 Avez-vous du sucre?
Have you any sugar?
J'ai acheté de la farine et de la margarine
I bought (some) flour and margarine
Il a mangé des gâteaux
He ate some cakes
Est-ce qu'il y a des lettres pour moi?
Are there (any) letters for me?

2 Il me doit de l'argent   **C'est de l'histoire ancienne**
He owes me (some) money   That's ancient history

3 Il a fait de gros efforts pour nous aider
He made a great effort to help us
Cette région a de belles églises
This region has some beautiful churches

4 des grandes vacances   **des jeunes gens**
summer holidays   young people

5 Je n'ai pas de nourriture/d'argent
I don't have any food/money
Vous n'avez pas de timbres/d'œufs?
Have you no stamps/eggs?
Je ne mange jamais de viande/d'omelettes
I never eat meat/omelettes
Il ne veut plus de visiteurs/d'eau
He doesn't want any more visitors/water

6 Il ne boit que du thé/de la bière/de l'eau
He only drinks tea/beer/water
Je n'ai que des problèmes avec cette machine
I have nothing but problems with this machine

The Indefinite Article

	WITH MASC. NOUN	WITH FEM. NOUN	
SING.	un	une	a
PLUR.	des	des	some

● **des** is also the plural of the partitive article (see p. 144)

● In negative sentences, **de** (**d'** + vowel) is used for both singular and plural (→ **1**)

● The indefinite article is used in French largely as it is in English EXCEPT:

  – there is no article when a person's profession is being stated (→ **2**) The article *is* present however, following **ce** (**c'** + vowel) (→ **3**)

  – the English article is not translated by **un/une** in constructions like *what a surprise, what an idiot* (→ **4**)

  – in structures of the type given in example **5** the article **un/une** is used in French and not translated in English (→ **5**)

1 Je n'ai pas de livre/d'enfants
I don't have a book/(any) children

2 Il est professeur   **Ma mère est infirmière**
He's a teacher   My mother's a nurse

3 C'est un médecin
He's/She's a doctor
Ce sont des acteurs
They're actors

4 Quelle surprise!   **Quel dommage!**
What a surprise!   What a shame!

5 avec une grande sagesse/un courage admirable
with great wisdom/admirable courage
Il a fait preuve d'un sang-froid incroyable
He showed incredible coolness
Un produit d'une qualité incomparable
A product of incomparable quality

Adjectives

Most adjectives agree in number and in gender with the noun or pronoun.

The formation of feminines

- Most adjectives add an **e** to the masculine singular form (→ **1**)

- If the masculine singular form already ends in **-e**, no further **e** is added (→ **2**)

- Some adjectives undergo a further change when **e** is added. These changes occur regularly and are shown on p. 150

- Irregular feminine forms are shown on p. 152

The formation of plurals

- The plural of both regular and irregular adjectives is formed by adding an **s** to the masculine or feminine singular form, as appropriate (→ **3**)

- When the masculine singular form already ends in **-s** or **-x**, no further **s** is added (→ **4**)

- For masculine singulars ending in **-au** and **-eau**, the masculine plural is **-aux** and **-eaux** (→ **5**)

- For masculine singulars ending in **-al**, the masculine plural is **-aux** (→ **6**)

  Exceptions: **final**   (masculine plural **finals**)
                   fatal   (masculine plural **fatals**)
                   naval   (masculine plural **navals**)

Pronunciation of feminine and plural adjectives
This is dealt with on p. 244

1 **mon frère aîné**   **ma sœur aînée**
my elder brother   my elder sister
le petit garçon   **la petite fille**
the little boy   the little girl
un sac gris   **une chemise grise**
a grey bag   a grey shirt
un bruit fort   **une voix forte**
a loud noise   a loud voice

2 **un jeune homme**   **une jeune femme**
a young man   a young woman
l'autre verre   **l'autre assiette**
the other glass   the other plate

3 **le dernier train**   **les derniers trains**
the last train   the last trains
une vieille maison   **de vieilles maisons**
an old house   old houses
un long voyage   **de longs voyages**
a long journey   long journeys
la rue étroite   **les rues étroites**
the narrow street   the narrow streets

4 **un diplomate français**   **des diplomates français**
a French diplomat   French diplomats
un homme dangereux   **des hommes dangereux**
a dangerous man   dangerous men

5 **le nouveau professeur**   **les nouveaux professeurs**
the new teacher   the new teachers
un chien esquimau   **des chiens esquimaux**
a husky (Fr. = an Eskimo dog) huskies (Fr. = Eskimo dogs)

6 **un ami loyal**   **des amis loyaux**
a loyal friend   loyal friends
un geste amical   **des gestes amicaux**
a friendly gesture   friendly gestures

Regular feminine endings

MASC. SING.	FEM. SING.	EXAMPLES	
-f	-ve	neuf, vif	(→ 1)
-x	-se	heureux, jaloux	(→ 2)
-eur	-euse	travailleur, flâneur	(→ 3)
-teur	{ -teuse	flatteur, menteur	(→ 4)
	{ -trice	destructeur, séducteur	(→ 5)

Exceptions:

bref: see p. 152

doux, faux, roux, vieux: see p. 152

extérieur, inférieur, intérieur, meilleur, supérieur: all add **e** to the masculine

enchanteur: fem. = **enchanteresse**

MASC. SING.	FEM. SING.	EXAMPLES	
-an	-anne	paysan	(→ 6)
-en	-enne	ancien, parisien	(→ 7)
-on	-onne	bon, breton	(→ 8)
-as	-asse	bas, las	(→ 9)
-et*	-ette	muet, violet	(→ 10)
-el	-elle	annuel, mortel	(→ 11)
-eil	-eille	pareil, vermeil	(→ 12)

Exception:

ras: fem. = **rase**

MASC. SING.	FEM. SING.	EXAMPLES	
-et*	-ète	secret, complet	(→ 13)
-er	-ère	étranger, fier	(→ 14)

*Note that there are two feminine endings for masculine adjectives ending in **-et**.

1 **un résultat positif**
a positive result

une attitude positive
a positive attitude

2 **d'un ton sérieux**
in a serious tone (of voice)

une voix sérieuse
a serious voice

3 **un enfant trompeur**
a deceitful child

une déclaration trompeuse
a misleading statement

4 **un tableau flatteur**
a flattering picture

une comparaison flatteuse
a flattering comparison

5 **un geste protecteur**
a protective gesture

une couche protectrice
a protective layer

6 **un problème paysan**
a farming problem

la vie paysanne
country life

7 **un avion égyptien**
an Egyptian plane

une statue égyptienne
an Egyptian statue

8 **un bon repas**
a good meal

de bonne humeur
in a good mood

9 **un plafond bas**
a low ceiling

à voix basse
in a low voice

10 **un travail net**
a clean piece of work

une explication nette
a clear explanation

11 **un homme cruel**
a cruel man

une remarque cruelle
a cruel remark

12 **un livre pareil**
such a book

en pareille occasion
on such an occasion

13 **un regard inquiet**
an anxious look

une attente inquiète
an anxious wait

14 **un goût amer**
a bitter taste

une amère déception
a bitter disappointment

Adjectives with irregular feminine forms

MASC. SING.	FEM. SING.		
aigu	aiguë	sharp; high-pitched	(→ 1)
ambigu	ambiguë	ambiguous	
beau (bel)*	belle	beautiful	
bénin	bénigne	benign	
blanc	blanche	white	
bref	brève	brief, short	(→ 2)
doux	douce	soft; sweet	
épais	épaisse	think	
esquimau	esquimaude	Eskimo	
faux	fausse	wrong	
favori	favorite	favourite	(→ 3)
fou (fol)*	folle	mad	
frais	fraîche	fresh	(→ 4)
franc	franche	frank	
gentil	gentille	kind	
grec	grecque	Greek	
gros	grosse	big	
jumeau	jumelle	twin	(→ 5)
long	longue	long	
malin	maligne	malignant	
mou (mol)*	molle	soft	
nouveau (nouvel)*	nouvelle	new	
nul	nulle	no	
public	publique	public	(→ 6)
roux	rousse	red-haired	
sec	sèche	dry	
sot	sotte	foolish	
turc	turque	Turkish	
vieux (vieil)*	vieille	old	

*This form is used when the following word begins with a vowel or an h 'mute' (→ 7)

1 **un son aigu**
   a high-pitched sound

   une douleur aiguë
   a sharp pain

2 **un bref discours**
   a short speech

   une brève rencontre
   a short meeting

3 **mon sport favori**
   my favourite sport

   ma chanson favorite
   my favourite song

4 **du pain frais**
   fresh bread

   de la crème fraîche
   fresh cream

5 **mon frère jumeau**
   my twin brother

   ma sœur jumelle
   my twin sister

6 **un jardin public**
   a (public) park

   l'opinion publique
   public opinion

7 **un bel appartement**
   a beautiful flat
   le nouvel inspecteur
   the new inspector
   un vieil arbre
   an old tree

   un bel habit
   a beautiful outfit
   un nouvel harmonica
   a new harmonica
   un vieil hôtel
   an old hotel

Comparatives and Superlatives

Comparatives
These are formed using the following constructions:

plus ... (que)	*more ... (than)*	(→ **1**)
moins ... (que)	*less ... (than)*	(→ **2**)
aussi ... que	*as ... as*	(→ **3**)
si ... que*	*as ... as*	(→ **4**)

*used mainly after a negative

Superlatives
These are formed using the following constructions:

le/la/les plus ... (que)	*the most ... (that)*	(→ **5**)
le/la/les moins ... (que)	*the least ... (that)*	(→ **6**)

● When the possessive adjective is present, two constructions are possible (→ **7**)
● After a superlative the preposition **de** is often translated as *in* (→ **8**)
● If a clause follows a superlative, the verb is in the subjunctive (→ **9**)

Adjectives with irregular comparatives/superlatives

ADJECTIVE	COMPARATIVE	SUPERLATIVE
bon	meilleur	le meilleur
good	*better*	*the best*
mauvais	pire OR	le pire OR
bad	plus mauvais	le plus mauvais
	worse	*the worst*
petit	moindre* OR	le moindre* OR
small	plus petit	le plus petit
	smaller;	*the smallest;*
	lesser	*the least*

*used only with abstract nouns

● Comparative and superlative adjectives agree in number and in gender with the noun, just like any other adjective (→ **10**)

1 **une raison plus grave**
   a more serious reason
   Elle est plus petite que moi
   She is smaller than me

2 **un film moins connu**
   a less well-known film
   C'est moins cher qu'il ne pense
   It's cheaper than he thinks

3 **Robert était aussi inquiet que moi**
   Robert was as worried as I was
   Cette ville n'est pas aussi grande que Bordeaux
   This town isn't as big as Bordeaux

4 **Ils ne sont pas si contents que ça**
   They aren't as happy as all that

5 **le guide le plus utile**   **la voiture la plus petite**
   the most useful guidebook   the smallest car
   les plus grandes maisons
   the biggest houses

6 **le mois le moins agréable**   **la fille la moins forte**
   the least pleasant month   the weakest girl
   les moins belles peintures
   the least attractive paintings

7 **Mon désir le plus cher** ⎫
   Mon plus cher désir ⎭ **est de voyager**
   My dearest wish is to travel

8 **la plus grande gare de Londres**
   the biggest station in London
   l'habitant le plus âgé du village/de la région
   the oldest inhabitant in the village/in the area

9 **la personne la plus gentille que je connaisse**
   the nicest person I know

10 **les moindres difficultés**
   the least difficulties
   la meilleure qualité
   the best quality

Demonstrative Adjectives

	MASCULINE	FEMININE	
SING.	ce (cet)	cette	*this; that*
PLUR.	ces	ces	*these; those*

● Demonstrative adjectives agree in number and gender with the noun (→ **1**)

● **cet** is used when the following word begins with a vowel or an **h** 'mute' (→ **2**)

● For emphasis or in order to distinguish between people or objects, **-ci** or **-là** is added to the noun: **-ci** indicates proximity (usually translated *this*) and **là** distance (*that*) (→ **3**)

1 Ce stylo ne marche pas
This/That pen isn't working
Comment s'appelle cette entreprise?
What's this/that company called?
Ces livres sont les miens
These/Those books are mine
Ces couleurs sont plus jolies
These/Those colours are nicer

2 cet oiseau
this/that bird
cet article
this/that article
cet homme
this/that man

3 Combien coûte ce manteau-ci?
How much is this coat?
Je voudrais cinq de ces pommes-là
I'd like five of those apples
Est-ce que tu reconnais cette personne-là?
Do you recognize that person?
Mettez ces vêtements-ci dans cette valise-là
Put these clothes in that case
Ce garçon-là appartient à ce groupe-ci
That boy belongs to this group

Interrogative Adjectives

	MASCULINE	FEMININE	
SING.	quel?	quelle?	what?; which?
PLUR.	quels?	quelles?	what?; which?

● Interrogative adjectives agree in number and gender with the noun
  (→ 1)

● The forms shown above are also used in indirect questions (→ 2)

Exclamatory Adjectives

	MASCULINE	FEMININE	
SING.	quel!	quelle!	what (a)!
PLUR.	quels!	quelles!	what!

● Exclamatory adjectives agree in number and gender with the noun
  (→ 3)

● For other exclamations, see p. 214

1 Quel genre d'homme est-ce?
What type of man is he?
Quelle est leur décision?
What is their decision?
Vous jouez de quels instruments?
What instruments do you play?
Quelles offres avez-vous reçues?
What offers have you received?
Quel vin recommandez-vous?
Which wine do you recommend?
Quelles couleurs préférez-vous?
Which colours do you prefer?

2 Je ne sais pas à quelle heure il est arrivé
I don't know what time he arrived
Dites-moi quels sont les livres les plus intéressants
Tell me which books are the most interesting

3 Quel dommage!
What a pity!
Quelle idée!
What an idea!
Quels beaux livres vous avez!
What fine books you have!
Quelles jolies fleurs!
What nice flowers!

Possessive Adjectives

WITH SING. NOUN		WITH PLUR. NOUN	
MASC.	FEM.	MASC./FEM.	
mon	ma (mon)	mes	my
ton	ta (ton)	tes	your
son	sa (son)	ses	his; her; its
notre	notre	nos	our
votre	votre	vos	your
leur	leur	leurs	their

● Possessive adjectives agree in number and gender with the noun, NOT WITH THE OWNER (→ 1)

● The forms shown in brackets are used when the following word begins with a vowel or an **h** 'mute' (→ 2)

● **son, sa, ses** have the additional meaning of *one's* (→ 3)

1 **Catherine a oublié son parapluie**
   Catherine has left her umbrella
   Paul cherche sa montre
   Paul's looking for his watch
   Mon frère et ma sœur habitent à Glasgow
   My brother and sister live in Glasgow
   Est-ce que tes voisins ont vendu leur voiture?
   Did your neighbours sell their car?
   Rangez vos affaires
   Put your things away

2 **mon appareil-photo**
   my camera
   ton histoire
   your story
   son erreur
   his/her mistake
   mon autre sœur
   my other sister

3 **perdre son équilibre**
   to lose one's balance
   présenter ses excuses
   to offer one's apologies

Position of Adjectives

- French adjectives usually follow the noun (→ **1**)

- Adjectives of colour or nationality *always* follow the noun (→ **2**)

- As in English, demonstrative, possessive, numerical and interrogative adjectives precede the noun (→ **3**)

- The adjectives **autre** *other* and **chaque** *each, every* precede the noun (→ **4**)

- The following common adjectives can precede the noun:

beau	*beautiful*	**jeune**	*young*
bon	*good*	**joli**	*pretty*
court	*short*	**long**	*long*
dernier	*last*	**mauvais**	*bad*
grand	*great*	**petit**	*small*
gros	*big*	**tel**	*such (a)*
haut	*high*	**vieux**	*old*

- The meaning of the following adjectives varies according to their position:

	BEFORE NOUN	AFTER NOUN	
ancien	*former*	*old, ancient*	(→ **5**)
brave	*good*	*brave*	(→ **6**)
cher	*dear (beloved)*	*expensive*	(→ **7**)
grand	*great*	*tall*	(→ **8**)
même	*same*	*very*	(→ **9**)
pauvre	*poor (wretched)*	*poor (not rich)*	(→ **10**)
propre	*own*	*clean*	(→ **11**)
seul	*single, sole*	*on one's own*	(→ **12**)
simple	*mere, simple*	*simple, easy*	(→ **13**)
vrai	*real*	*true*	(→ **14**)

- Adjectives following the noun are linked by **et** (→ **15**)

1 **le chapitre suivant**
the following chapter

l'heure exacte
the right time

2 **une cravate rouge**
a red tie

un mot français
a French word

3 **ce dictionnaire**
this dictionary

mon père
my father

le premier étage
the first floor

deux exemples
two examples

quel homme?
which man?

4 **une autre fois**
another time

chaque jour
every day

5 **un ancien collègue**
a former colleague

l'histoire ancienne
ancient history

6 **un brave homme**
a good man

un homme brave
a brave man

7 **mes chers amis**
my dear friends

une robe chère
an expensive dress

8 **un grand peintre**
a great painter

un homme grand
a tall man

9 **la même réponse**
the same answer

vos paroles mêmes
your very words

10 **cette pauvre femme**
that poor woman

une nation pauvre
a poor nation

11 **ma propre vie**
my own life

une chemise propre
a clean shirt

12 **une seule réponse**
a single reply

une femme seule
a woman on her own

13 **un simple regard**
a mere look

un problème simple
a simple problem

14 **la vraie raison**
the real reason

les faits vrais
the true facts

15 **un acte lâche et trompeur**
a cowardly, deceitful act
un acte lâche, trompeur et ignoble
a cowardly, deceitful and ignoble act

Personal Pronouns

SUBJECT PRONOUNS

PERSON	SINGULAR	PLURAL
1st	**je (j')**	**nous**
	I	we
2nd	**tu**	**vous**
	you	you
3rd (masc.)	**il**	**ils**
	he; it	they
(fem.)	**elle**	**elles**
	she; it	they

je changes to **j'** before a vowel, an **h** 'mute', or the pronoun **y** (→ **1**)

- **tu/vous**
  Vous, as well as being the second person plural, is also used when addressing one person. As a general rule, use **tu** only when addressing a friend, a child, a relative, someone you know very well, or when invited to do so. In all other cases use **vous**. For singular and plural uses of **vous**, see example **2**.

- **il/elle; ils/elles**
  The form of the 3rd person pronouns reflects the number and gender of the noun(s) they replace, referring to animals and things as well as to people. **Ils** also replaces a combination of masculine and feminine nouns (→ **3**)

- Sometimes stressed pronouns replace the subject pronouns, see p. 172

Continued

1 J'arrive!
I'm just coming!
J'en ai trois
I've got 3 of them
J'hésite à le déranger
I hesitate to disturb him
J'y pense souvent
I often think about it

2 Compare: **Vous êtes certain, Monsieur Leclerc?**
Are you sure, Mr Leclerc?
and: **Vous êtes certains, les enfants?**
Are you sure, children?

Compare: **Vous êtes partie quand, Estelle?**
When did you leave, Estelle?
and: **Estelle et Sophie – vous êtes parties quand?**
Estelle and Sophie – when did you leave?

3 Où logent ton père et ta mère quand ils vont à Rome?
Where do your father and mother stay when they go to Rome?
Donne-moi le journal et les lettres quand ils arriveront
Give me the newspaper and the letters when they arrive

Personal Pronouns (ctd.)

DIRECT OBJECT PRONOUNS

PERSON	SINGULAR	PLURAL
1st	**me (m')**	**nous**
	me	*us*
2nd	**te (t')**	**vous**
	you	*you*
3rd (masc.)	**le (l')**	**les**
	him; it	*them*
(fem.)	**la (l')**	**les**
	her; it	*them*

The forms shown in brackets are used before a vowel, an **h** 'mute', or the pronoun **y** (→ **1**)

● In positive commands **me** and **te** change to **moi** and **toi** except before **en** or **y** (→ **2**)

● **le** sometimes functions as a 'neuter' pronoun, referring to an idea or information contained in a previous statement or question. It is often not translated (→ **3**)

Position of direct object pronouns

● In constructions other than the imperative affirmative the pronoun comes before the verb (→ **4**)

The same applies when the verb is in the infinitive (→ **5**)

In the imperative affirmative, the pronoun follows the verb and is attached to it by a hyphen (→ **6**)

● For further information, see Order of Object Pronouns, p. 170

Reflexive Pronouns

These are dealt with under reflexive verbs, p. 30

Continued

1 Il m'a vu
He saw me
Je ne t'oublierai jamais
I'll never forget you
Ça l'habitue à travailler seul
That gets him/her used to working on his/her own
Je veux l'y accoutumer
I want to accustom him/her to it

2 Avertis-moi de ta décision → Avertis-m'en
Inform me of your decision   Inform me of it

3 Il n'est pas là. – Je le sais bien.
He isn't there. – I know that.
Aidez-moi si vous le pouvez
Help me if you can
Elle viendra demain. – Je l'espère bien.
She'll come tomorrow. – I hope so.

4 Je t'aime
I love you
Les voyez-vous?
Can you see them?
Elle ne nous connaît pas
She doesn't know us
Est-ce que tu ne les aimes pas?
Don't you like them?
Ne me faites pas rire
Don't make me laugh

5 Puis-je vous aider?
May I help you?

6 Aidez-moi   **Suivez-nous**
Help me   Follow us

Personal Pronouns (ctd.)

INDIRECT OBJECT PRONOUNS

PERSON	SINGULAR	PLURAL
1st	me (m')	nous
2nd	te (t')	vous
3rd (masc.)	lui	leur
(fem.)	lui	leur

me and te change to m' and t' before a vowel or an h 'mute'
(→1)

● In positive commands, me and te change to moi and toi except
before en (→2)

● The pronouns shown in the above table replace the preposition à +
noun, where the noun is a person or an animal (→3)

● The verbal construction affects the translation of the pronoun (→4)

Position of indirect object pronouns

● In constructions other than the imperative affirmative, the pronoun
comes before the verb (→5)
The same applies when the verb is in the infinitive (→6)
In the imperative affirmative, the pronoun follows the verb and is
attached to it by a hyphen (→7)

● For further information, see Order of Object Pronouns, p. 170

Reflexive Pronouns

These are dealt with under reflexive verbs, p. 30

Continued

1 **Tu m'as donné ce livre**
You gave me this book
Ils t'ont caché les faits
They hid the facts from you

2 **Donnez-moi du sucre** → **Donnez-m'en**
Give me some sugar   Give me some
Garde-toi assez d'argent → **Garde-t'en assez**
Keep enough money for   Keep enough for yourself
yourself

3 **J'écris à Suzanne** → **Je lui écris**
I'm writing to Suzanne   I'm writing to her
Donne du lait au chat → **Donne-lui du lait**
Give the cat some milk   Give it some milk

4 **arracher qch à qn**   to snatch sth from sb:
    Un voleur m'a arraché mon porte-monnaie
    A thief snatched my purse from me
promettre qch à qn   to promise sb sth:
    Il leur a promis un cadeau
    He promised them a present
demander à qn de faire   to ask sb to do:
    Elle nous avait demandé de revenir
    She had asked us to come back

5 **Elle vous a écrit**   **Vous a-t-elle écrit?**
She's written to you   Has she written to you?
Il ne nous parle pas
He doesn't speak to us
Est-ce que cela ne vous intéresse pas?
Doesn't it interest you?
Ne leur répondez pas
Don't answer them

6 **Voulez-vous leur envoyer l'adresse?**
Do you want to send them the address?

7 **Répondez-moi**   **Donnez-nous la réponse**
Answer me   Tell us the answer

Personal Pronouns (ctd.)

Order of object pronouns

- When two object pronouns of different persons come before the verb, the order is: indirect before direct, i.e.

$$
\left.\begin{array}{c} \textbf{me} \\ \textbf{te} \\ \textbf{nous} \\ \textbf{vous} \end{array}\right\} \text{ before } \left\{\begin{array}{c} \textbf{le} \\ \textbf{la} \\ \textbf{les} \end{array}\right. \quad (\rightarrow \textbf{1})
$$

- When two 3rd person object pronouns come before the verb, the order is: direct before indirect, i.e.

$$
\left.\begin{array}{c} \textbf{le} \\ \textbf{la} \\ \textbf{les} \end{array}\right\} \text{ before } \left\{\begin{array}{c} \textbf{lui} \\ \textbf{leur} \end{array}\right. \quad (\rightarrow \textbf{2})
$$

- When two object pronouns come after the verb (i.e. in the imperative affirmative), the order is: direct before indirect, i.e.

$$
\left.\begin{array}{c} \textbf{le} \\ \textbf{la} \\ \textbf{les} \end{array}\right\} \text{ before } \left\{\begin{array}{c} \textbf{moi} \\ \textbf{toi} \\ \textbf{lui} \\ \textbf{nous} \\ \textbf{vous} \\ \textbf{leur} \end{array}\right. \quad (\rightarrow \textbf{3})
$$

- The pronouns **y** and **en** (see pp. 176 and 174) always come last (→ **4**)

Continued

1 Dominique vous l'envoie demain
Dominique's sending it to you tomorrow
Est-ce qu'il te les a montrés?
Has he shown them to you?
Ne me le dis pas
Don't tell me (it)
Il ne veut pas nous la prêter
He won't lend it to us

2 Elle le leur a emprunté
She borrowed it from them
Je les lui ai lus
I read them to him/her
Ne la leur donne pas
Don't give it to them
Je voudrais les lui rendre
I'd like to give them back to him/her

3 Rends-les-moi
Give them back to me
Donnez-le-nous
Give it to us
Apportons-les-leur
Let's take them to them

4 Donnez-leur-en
Give them some
Je l'y ai déposé
I dropped him there
Ne nous en parlez plus
Don't speak to us about it any more

Personal Pronouns (ctd.)

STRESSED OR DISJUNCTIVE PRONOUNS

PERSON	SINGULAR	PLURAL
1st	**moi**	**nous**
	me	*us*
2nd	**toi**	**vous**
	you	*you*
3rd (masc.)	**lui**	**eux**
	him; it	*them*
(fem.)	**elle**	**elles**
	her; it	*them*
('reflexive')	**soi**	
	oneself	

● These pronouns are used:
  – after prepositions (→ **1**)
  – on their own (→ **2**)
  – following **c'est**, **ce sont** *it is* (→ **3**)
  – for emphasis, especially where contrast is involved (→ **4**)
  – when the subject consists of two or more pronouns (→ **5**)
  – when the subject consists of a pronoun and a noun (→ **6**)
  – in comparisons (→ **7**)
  – before relative pronouns (→ **8**)

● For particular emphasis **-même** (singular) or **-mêmes** (plural) is
  added to the pronoun (→ **9**)

moi-même	*myself*	**nous-mêmes**	*ourselves*
toi-même	*yourself*	**vous-même**	*yourself*
lui-même	*himself; itself*	**vous-mêmes**	*yourselves*
elle-même	*herself; itself*	**eux-mêmes**	*themselves*
soi-même	*oneself*	**elles-mêmes**	*themselves*

1 **Je pense à toi**
  I think about you
  C'est pour elle
  This is for her
  Venez avec moi
  Come with me

  Partez sans eux
  Leave without them
  Assieds-toi à côté de lui
  Sit beside him
  Il a besoin de nous
  He needs us

2 **Qui a fait cela? – Lui.**
  Who did that? – He did.
  Qui est-ce qui gagne? – Moi
  Who's winning? – Me

3 **C'est toi, Simon? – Non, c'est moi, David.**
  Is that you, Simon? – No, it's me, David
  Qui est-ce? – Ce sont eux.
  Who is it? – It's them.

4 **Ils voyagent séparément: lui par le train, elle en autobus**
  They travel separately: he by train and she by bus
  Toi, tu ressembles à ton père, eux pas
  You look like your father, *they* don't
  Il n'a pas l'air de s'ennuyer, lui!
  He doesn't look bored!

5 **Lui et moi partons demain**
  He and I are leaving tomorrow
  Ni vous ni elles ne pouvez rester
  Neither you nor they can stay

6 **Mon père et elle ne s'entendent pas**
  My father and she don't get on

7 **plus jeune que moi**
  younger than me

  Il est moins grand que toi
  He's smaller than you (are)

8 **Moi, qui étais malade, je n'ai pas pu les accompagner**
  I, who was ill, couldn't go with them
  Ce sont eux qui font du bruit, pas nous
  They're the ones making the noise, not us

9 **Je l'ai fait moi-même**
  I did it myself

The pronoun en

- **en** replaces the preposition **de** + noun (→ **1**)
  The verbal construction can affect the translation (→ **2**)

- **en** also replaces the partitive article (*English = some, any*) + noun
  (→ **3**)

In expressions of quantity **en** represents the noun (→ **4**)

- Position:
  en comes before the verb, except in positive commands when it
  follows and is attached to the verb by a hyphen (→ **5**)

- **en** follows other object pronouns (→ **6**)

1 **Il est fier de son succès** → **Il en est fier**
  He's proud of his success   He's proud of it
  Elle est sortie du cinéma → **Elle en est sortie**
  She came out of the cinema She came out (of it)
  Je suis couvert de peinture → **J'en suis couvert**
  I'm covered in paint   I'm covered in it
  Il a beaucoup d'amis → **Il en a beaucoup**
  He has lots of friends   He has lots (of them)

2 **avoir besoin de qch** to need sth:
    J'en ai besoin
    I need it/them
  avoir peur de qch to be afraid of sth:
    J'en ai peur
    I'm afraid of it/them

3 **Avez-vous de l'argent?** → **En avez-vous?**
  Have you any money?   Do you have any?
  Je veux acheter des timbres → **Je veux en acheter**
  I want to buy some stamps I want to buy some

4 **J'ai deux crayons** → **J'en ai deux**
  I've two pencils   I've two (of them)
  Combien de sœurs as-tu? – J'en ai trois.
  How many sisters do you have? – I have three.

5 **Elle en a discuté avec moi**
  She discussed it with me
  En êtes-vous content?
  Are you pleased with
  it/them?
  Je veux en garder trois
  I want to keep three of them
  N'en parlez plus
  Don't talk about it any more
  Prenez-en   **Soyez-en fier**
  Take some   Be proud of it/them

6 **Donnez-leur-en**   **Il m'en a parlé**
  Give them some   He spoke to me about it

The pronoun y

● **y** replaces the preposition **à** + noun (→ **1**)
  The verbal construction can affect the translation (→ **2**)

● **y** also replaces the prepositions **dans** and **sur** + noun (→ **3**)

● **y** can also mean *there* (→ **4**)

● Position:
  y comes before the verb, except in positive commands when it follows and is attached to the verb by a hyphen (→ **5**)

● **y** follows other object pronouns (→ **6**)

1 Ne touchez pas à ce bouton → **N'y touchez pas**
Don't touch this switch   Don't touch it
Il participe aux concerts → **Il y participe**
He takes part in the concerts   He takes part (in them)

2 **penser à qch** to think about sth:
   J'y pense souvent
   I often think about it
consentir à qch to agree to sth:
   Tu y as consenti?
   Have you agreed to it?

3 Mettez-les dans la boîte → **Mettez-les-y**
Put them in the box   Put them in it
Il les a mis sur les étagères → **Il les y a mis**
He put them on the shelves   He put them on them
J'ai placé de l'argent sur ce
compte → **J'y ai placé de l'argent**
I've put money into this   I've put money into it
account

4 **Elle y passe tout l'été**
She spends the whole summer there

5 **Il y a ajouté du sucre**
He added sugar to it
Elle n'y a pas écrit son nom
She hasn't written her name on it
Comment fait-on pour y aller?
How do you get there?
N'y pense plus!
Don't give it another thought!
Restez-y   **Réfléchissez-y**
Stay there   Think it over

6 **Elle m'y a conduit**   **Menez-nous-y**
She drove me there   Take us there

Indefinite Pronouns

aucun(e)	*none, not any*	(→1)
certain(e)s	*some, certain*	(→2)
chacun(e)	*each (one)*	(→3)
	everybody	
on	*one, you*	
	somebody	
	they, people	(→4)
	we (informal use)	
personne	*nobody*	(→5)
plusieurs	*several*	(→6)
quelque chose	*something; anything*	(→7)
quelques-un(e)s	*some, a few*	(→8)
quelqu'un	*somebody; anybody*	(→9)
rien	*nothing*	(→10)
tout	*all; everything*	(→11)
tous (toutes)	*all*	(→12)
l'un(e) ... l'autre	*(the) one ... the other*	
les un(e)s ... les autres	*some ...others*	(→13)

● **aucun(e), personne, rien**

When used as subject or object of the verb, these require the word **ne** placed immediately before the verb. Note that **aucun** further needs the pronoun **en** when used as an object (→14)

● **quelque chose, rien**

When qualified by an adjective, these pronouns require the preposition **de** before the adjective (→15)

1 Combien en avez-vous? – Aucun
How many have you got? – None

2 Certains pensent que ...
Some (people) think that ...

3 Chacune de ces boîtes est pleine   **Chacun son tour!**
Each of these boxes is full   Everybody in turn!

4 On voit l'église de cette fenêtre
You can see the church from this window
À la campagne on se couche tôt
In the country they/we go to bed early
Est-ce qu'on lui a permis de rester?
Was he/she allowed to stay?

5 Qui voyez-vous? – Personne
Who can you see? – Nobody

6 Ils sont plusieurs
There are several of them

7 Mange donc quelque chose!   **Tu as vu quelque chose?**
Eat something!   Did you see anything?

8 Je connais quelques-uns de ses amis
I know some of his/her friends

9 Quelqu'un a appelé   **Tu as vu quelqu'un?**
Somebody called (out)   Did you see anybody?

10 Qu'est-ce que tu as dans la main? – Rien
What have you got in your hand? – Nothing

11 Il a tout gâché   **Tout va bien**
He has spoiled everything   All's well

12 Tu les as tous?   **Elles sont toutes venues**
Do you have all of them?   They all came

13 Les uns sont satisfaits, les autres pas
Some are satisfied, (the) others aren't

14 Je ne vois personne   **Rien ne lui plaît**
I can't see anyone   Nothing pleases him/her
Aucune des entreprises ne veut ...   **Il n'en a aucun**
None of the companies wants ...   He hasn't any (of them)

15 quelque chose de grand   **rien d'intéressant**
something big   nothing interesting

Relative Pronouns

qui   *who; which*
que   *who(m); which*

These are subject and direct object pronouns that introduce a clause and refer to people or things.

	PEOPLE	THINGS
SUBJECT	**qui** (→1)	**qui** (→3)
	who, that	*which, that*
DIRECT OBJECT	**que (qu')** (→2)	**que (qu')** (→4)
	who(m), that	*which, that*

● **que** changes to **qu'** before a vowel (→**2/4**)
● You cannot omit the object relative pronoun in French as you can in English (→**2/4**)

After a preposition:
● When referring to people, use **qui** (→**5**)
    Exceptions: after **parmi** *among* and **entre** *between* use **lesquels/lesquelles** (see below) (→**6**)
● When referring to things, use forms of **lequel**:

	MASCULINE	FEMININE	
SING.	**lequel**	**laquelle**	*which*
PLUR.	**lesquels**	**lesquelles**	*which*

The pronoun agrees in number and gender with the noun (→**7**)

● After the prepositions **à** and **de**, **lequel** and **lesquel(le)s** contract as follows:

$$à + lequel → auquel$$
$$à + lesquels → auxquels \qquad (→8)$$
$$à + lesquelles → auxquelles$$

$$de + lequel → duquel$$
$$de + lesquels → desquels \qquad (→9)$$
$$de + lesquelles → desquelles$$

Continued

1 **Mon frère, qui a vingt ans, est à l'université**
My brother, who's twenty, is at university

2 **Les amis que je vois le plus sont ...**
The friends (that) I see most are ...
Lucienne, qu'il connaît depuis longtemps, est ...
Lucienne, whom he has known for a long time, is ...

3 **Il y a un escalier qui mène au toît**
There's a staircase which leads to the roof

4 **La maison que nous avons achetée a ...**
The house (which) we've bought has ...
Voici le cadeau qu'elle m'a envoyé
This is the present (that) she sent me

5 **la personne à qui il parle**
the person he's talking to
la personne avec qui je voyage
the person with whom I travel
les enfants pour qui je l'ai acheté
the children for whom I bought it

6 **Il y avait des jeunes, parmi lesquels Robert**
There were some young people, Robert among them
les filles entre lesquelles j'étais assis
the girls between whom I was sitting

7 **le torchon avec lequel il l'essuie**
the cloth he's wiping it with
la table sur laquelle je l'ai mis
the table on which I put it
les moyens par lesquels il l'accomplit
the means by which he achieves it
les pièces pour lesquelles elle est connue
the plays for which she is famous

8 **le magasin auquel il livre ces marchandises**
the shop to which he delivers these goods

9 **les injustices desquelles il se plaint**
the injustices he's complaining about

Relative Pronouns (ctd.)

quoi   *which, what*

● When the relative pronoun does not refer to a specific noun, **quoi** is used after a preposition (→**1**)

dont   *whose, of whom, of which*

● **dont** often (but not always) replaces **de qui, duquel, de laquelle**, and **desquel(le)s** (→**2**)

● It cannot replace **de qui, duquel** etc in the construction preposition + noun + **de qui/duquel** (→**3**)

Continued

1 C'est en quoi vous vous trompez
That's where you're wrong
A quoi, j'ai répondu '...'
To which I replied, '...'

2 la femme dont (= de qui) la voiture est garée en face
the woman whose car is parked opposite
un prix dont (= de qui) je suis fier
an award I am proud of
un ami dont (= de qui) je connais le frère
a friend whose brother I know
les enfants dont (= de qui) vous vous occupez
the children you look after
le film dont (= duquel) il a parlé
the film of which he spoke
la fenêtre dont (= de laquelle) les rideaux sont tirés
the window whose curtains are drawn
des livres dont (= desquels) j'ai oublié les titres
books whose titles I've forgotten
les maladies dont (= desquelles) il souffre
the illnesses he suffers from

3 une personne sur l'aide de qui on peut compter
a person whose help one can rely on
les enfants aux parents de qui j'écris
the children to whose parents I'm writing
la maison dans le jardin de laquelle il y a ...
the house in whose garden there is ...

Relative Pronouns (ctd.)

ce qui, ce que *that which, what*

These are used when the relative pronoun does not refer to a specific noun, and they are often translated as *what* (literally: *that which*)

> **ce qui** is used as the subject (→**1**)
> **ce que*** is used as the direct object (→**2**)
>
> ***que** changes to **qu'** before a vowel (→**2**)

● Note the construction
> **tout ce qui** ⎫
> **tout ce que** ⎭ *everything/all that* (→**3**)

● de + **ce que** → **ce dont** (→**4**)

● preposition + **ce que** → **ce** + preposition + **quoi** (→**5**)

● When **ce qui, ce que** etc, refers to a previous CLAUSE the translation is *which* (→**6**)

Continued

1 **Ce qui m'intéresse ne l'intéresse pas forcément**
What interests me doesn't necessarily interest him
Je n'ai pas vu ce qui s'est passé
I didn't see what happened

2 **Ce que j'aime c'est la musique classique**
What I like is classical music
Montrez-moi ce qu'il vous a donné
Show me what he gave you

3 **Tout ce qui reste c'est ...**
All that's left is ...
Donnez-moi tout ce que vous avez
Give me everything you have

4 **Il risque de perdre ce dont il est si fier**
He risks losing what he's so proud of
Voilà ce dont il s'agit
That's what it's about

5 **Ce n'est pas ce à quoi je m'attendais**
It's not what I was expecting
Ce à quoi je m'intéresse particulièrement c'est ...
What I'm particularly interested in is ...

6 **Il est d'accord, ce qui m'étonne**
He agrees, which surprises me
Il a dit qu'elle ne venait pas, ce que nous savions déjà
He said she wasn't coming, which we already knew

Interrogative Pronouns

qui? *who?; whom?*
que? *what?*
quoi? *what?*

These pronouns are used in direct questions.
The form of the pronoun depends on:
- whether it refers to people or to things
- whether it is the subject or object of the verb, or if it comes after a preposition

Qui and **que** have longer forms, as shown in the tables below.

- Referring to people:

SUBJECT	**qui?**	
	qui est-ce qui?	(→1)
	who?	
OBJECT	**qui?**	
	qui est-ce que*?	(→2)
	who(m)?	
AFTER PREPOSITIONS	**qui?**	(→3)
	who(m)?	

- Referring to things:

SUBJECT	**qu'est-ce qui?**	(→4)
	what?	
OBJECT	**que*?**	
	qu'est-ce que*?	(→5)
	what?	
AFTER PREPOSITIONS	**quoi?**	(→6)
	what?	

*que changes to **qu'** before a vowel (→2, 5)

Continued

1 Qui vient?
   Qui est-ce qui vient?
   Who's coming?

2 Qui vois-tu?
   Qui est-ce que tu vois?
   Who(m) can you see?
   Qui a-t-elle rencontré?
   Qui est-ce qu'elle a rencontré?
   Who(m) did she meet?

3 De qui parle-t-il?
   Who's he talking about?
   Pour qui est ce livre?
   Who's this book for?
   A qui avez-vous écrit?
   To whom did you write?

4 Qu'est-ce qui se passe?
   What's happening?
   Qu'est-ce qui a vexé Paul?
   What upset Paul?

5 Que faites-vous?
   Qu'est-ce que vous faites?
   What are you doing?
   Qu'a-t-il dit?
   Qu'est-ce qu'il a dit?
   What did he say?

6 A quoi cela sert-il?
   What's that used for?
   De quoi a-t-on parlé?
   What was the discussion about?
   Sur quoi vous basez-vous?
   What do you base it on?

Interrogative Pronouns (ctd.)

qui *who; whom*
ce qui *what*
ce que *what*
quoi *what*

These pronouns are used in indirect questions.
The form of the pronoun depends on:

  – whether it refers to people or to things
  – whether it is the subject or object of the verb, or if it comes
    after a preposition

● Referring to people: use **qui** in all instances (→**1**)

● Referring to things:

SUBJECT	**ce qui** *what*	(→**2**)
OBJECT	**ce que*** *what*	(→**3**)
AFTER PREPOSITIONS	**quoi** *what*	(→**4**)

  ***que** changes to **qu'** before a vowel (→**3**)

Continued

1 **Demande-lui qui est venu**
   Ask him who came
   Je me demande qui ils ont vu
   I wonder who they saw
   Dites-moi qui vous préférez
   Tell me who you prefer
   Elle ne sait pas à qui s'adresser
   She doesn't know who to apply to
   Demandez-leur pour qui elles travaillent
   Ask them who they work for

2 **Il se demande ce qui se passe**
   He's wondering what's happening
   Je ne sais pas ce qui vous fait croire que ...
   I don't know what makes you think that ...

3 **Raconte-nous ce que tu as fait**
   Tell us what you did
   Je me demande ce qu'elle pense
   I wonder what she's thinking

4 **On ne sait pas de quoi vivent ces animaux**
   We don't know what these animals live on
   Je vais lui demander à quoi il fait allusion
   I'm going to ask him what he's hinting at

Interrogative Pronouns (ctd.)

lequel?, laquelle?; lesquels?, lesquelles?

	MASCULINE	FEMININE	
SING.	**lequel?**	**laquelle?**	which (one)?
PLUR.	**lesquels?**	**lesquelles?**	which (ones)?

- The pronoun agrees in number and gender with the noun it refers to (→**1**)

- The same forms are used in indirect questions (→**2**)

- After the prepositions **à** and **de**, **lequel** and **lesquel(le)s** contract as follows:

  > **à + lequel? → auquel?**
  > **à + lesquels? → auxquels?**
  > **à + lesquelles? → auxquelles?**
  >
  > **de + lequel? → duquel?**
  > **de + lesquels? → desquels?**
  > **de + lesquelles? → desquelles?**

1 J'ai choisi un livre. – Lequel?
I've chosen a book. – Which one?
Laquelle de ces valises est la vôtre?
Which of these cases is yours?
Amenez quelques amis. – Lesquels?
Bring some friends. – Which ones?
Lesquelles de vos sœurs sont mariées?
Which of your sisters are married?

2 Je me demande laquelle des maisons est la leur
I wonder which is their house
Dites-moi lesquels d'entre eux étaient là
Tell me which of them were there

Possessive Pronouns

SINGULAR		
MASCULINE	*FEMININE*	
le mien	la mienne	*mine*
le tien	la tienne	*yours*
le sien	la sienne	*his; hers; its*
le nôtre	la nôtre	*ours*
le vôtre	la vôtre	*yours*
le leur	la leur	*theirs*

PLURAL		
MASCULINE	*FEMININE*	
les miens	les miennes	*mine*
les tiens	les tiennes	*yours*
les siens	les siennes	*his; hers; its*
les nôtres	les nôtres	*ours*
les vôtres	les vôtres	*yours*
les leurs	les leurs	*theirs*

- The pronoun agrees in number and gender with the noun it replaces, NOT WITH THE OWNER (→1)

- Alternative translations are *my own, your own* etc; **le sien, la sienne** etc. may also mean *one's own* (→2)

- After the prepositions **à** and **de** the articles **le** and **les** are contracted in the normal way (see p. 140):

à + le mien → au mien
    à + les miens → aux miens   (→3)
    à + les miennes → aux miennes

    de + le mien → du mien
    de + les miens → des miens   (→4)
    de + les miennes → des miennes

1 Demandez à Carole si ce stylo est le sien
Ask Carol if this pen is hers
Quelle équipe a gagné – la leur ou la nôtre?
Which team won – theirs or ours?
Mon stylo marche mieux que le tien
My pen writes better than yours
Richard a pris mes affaires pour les siennes
Richard mistook my belongings for his
Si tu n'as pas de disques, emprunte les miens
If you don't have any records, borrow mine
Nos maisons sont moins grandes que les vôtres
Our houses are smaller than yours

2 Est-ce que leur entreprise est aussi grande que la vôtre?
Is their company as big as your own?
Leurs prix sont moins élevés que les nôtres
Their prices are lower than our own
Le bonheur des autres importe plus que le sien
Other people's happiness matters more than one's own

3 Pourquoi préfères-tu ce manteau au mien?
Why do you prefer this coat to mine?
Quelles maisons ressemblent aux leurs?
Which houses resemble theirs?

4 Leur car est garé
Their coach is parked
Vos livres sont au-dessus des miens
Your books are on top of mine

Demonstrative Pronouns

celui, celle; ceux, celles

	MASCULINE	FEMININE	
SING.	**celui**	**celle**	*the one*
PLUR.	**ceux**	**celles**	*the ones*

● The pronoun agrees in number and gender with the noun it replaces (→**1**)

● Uses:
  – preceding a relative pronoun, meaning *the one(s) who/which* (→**1**)
  – preceding the preposition **de**, meaning *the one(s) belonging to, the one(s) of* (→**2**)
  – with **-ci** and **-là**, for emphasis or to distinguish between two things:

	MASCULINE	FEMININE		
SING.	**celui-ci**	**celle-ci**	*this (one)*	(→**3**)
PLUR.	**ceux-ci**	**celles-ci**	*these (ones)*	

	MASCULINE	FEMININE		
SING.	**celui-là**	**celle-là**	*that (one)*	(→**3**)
PLUR.	**ceux-là**	**celles-là**	*those (ones)*	

  – an additional meaning of **celui-ci/celui-là** etc. is *the former/the latter*

Continued

1 Lequel? – Celui qui parle à Anne
Which man? – The one who's talking to Anne
Quelle robe désirez-vous? – Celle qui est en vitrine
Which dress do you want? – The one which is in the window
Est-ce que ces livres sont ceux qu'il t'a donnés?
Are these the books that he gave you?
Quelles filles? – Celles que nous avons vues hier
Which girls? – The ones we saw yesterday
Cet article n'est pas celui dont vous m'avez parlé
This article isn't the one you spoke to me about

2 Ce jardin est plus grand que celui de mes parents
This garden is bigger than my parents' (garden)
Est-ce que ta fille est plus âgée que celle de Gabrielle?
Is your daughter older than Gabrielle's (daughter)?
Je préfère les enfants de Paul à ceux de Roger
I prefer Paul's children to Roger's (children)
Comparez vos réponses à celles de votre voisin
Compare your answers with your neighbours (answers)
les montagnes d'Écosse et celles du pays de Galles
the mountains of Scotland and those of Wales

3 Quel tailleur préférez-vous: celui-ci ou celui-là?
Which suit do you prefer: this one or that one?
Cette chemise a deux poches mais celle-là n'en a pas
This shirt has two pockets but that one has none
Quels œufs choisirais-tu: ceux-ci ou ceux-là?
Which eggs would you choose: these (ones) or those (ones)?
De toutes mes jupes, celle-ci me va le mieux
Of all my skirts, this one fits me best

Demonstrative Pronouns (ctd.)

ce (c') *it, that*

● Usually used with **être**, in the expressions **c'est**, **c'était**, **ce sont** etc. (→**1**)

● Note the spelling **ç** when followed by the letter **a** (→**2**)

● Uses:
  - to identify a person or object (→**3**)
  - for emphasis (→**4**)
  - as a neuter pronoun, referring to a statement, idea etc. (→**5**)

ce qui, ce que, ce dont etc.: see Relative Pronouns (p. 184), Interrogative Pronouns (p. 188)

cela, ça *it, that*

● **cela** and **ça** are used as 'neuter' pronouns, referring to a statement, an idea, an object (→**6**)

● In everyday spoken language **ça** is used in preference to **cela**

ceci *this* (→**7**)

● **ceci** is not used as often as 'this' in English; **cela**, **ça** are often used where we use 'this'

1 C'est...
It's/That's...

C'était moi
It was me

2 Ç'a été la cause de...
It has been cause of...

3 Qui est-ce?
Who is it?; Who's this/that?; Who's he/she?
C'est lui/mon frère/nous
It's/That's him/my brother/us
C'est une infirmière*
She's a nurse
Qu'est-ce que c'est?
What's this/that?
C'est une agrafeuse
It's a stapler

Ce sont eux
It's them
Ce sont des professeurs*
They're teachers
Qu'est-ce que c'est que ça?
What's that?
Ce sont des trombones
They're paper clips

4 C'est moi qui ai téléphoné
It was me who phoned
Ce sont les enfants qui importent le plus
It's the children who matter most

5 C'est très intéressant
That's/It's very interesting
Ce serait dangereux
That/It would be dangerous

6 Ça ne fait rien
It doesn't matter
A quoi bon faire ça?
What's the use of doing that?
Cela ne compte pas
That doesn't count
Cela demande du temps
It/That takes time

7 A qui est ceci?
Whose is this?

Ouvrez-le comme ceci
Open it like this

*See pp. 146 and 147 for the use of the article when stating a person's profession

Adverbs

Formation

- Most adverbs are formed by adding **-ment** to the feminine form of the adjective (→**1**)

- **-ment** is added to the *masculine* form when the masculine form ends in **-é**, **-i** or **-u** (→**2**)
  Exception: **gai** (→**3**)
  Occasionally the **u** changes to **û** before **-ment** is added (→**4**)

- If the adjective ends in **-ant** or **-ent**, the adverb ends in **-amment** or **-emment** (→**5**)
  Exceptions: **lent**, **présent** (→**6**)

Irregular Adverbs

ADJECTIVE		ADVERB		
aveugle	*blind*	**aveuglément**	blindly	
bon	*good*	**bien**	well	(→**7**)
bref	*brief*	**brièvement**	briefly	
énorme	*enormous*	**énormément**	enormously	
exprès	*express*	**expressément**	expressly	(→**8**)
gentil	*kind*	**gentiment**	kindly	
mauvais	*bad*	**mal**	badly	(→**9**)
meilleur	*better*	**mieux**	better	
pire	*worse*	**pis**	worse	
précis	*precise*	**précisément**	precisely	
profond	*deep*	**profondément**	deeply	(→**10**)
traître	*treacherous*	**traîtreusement**	treacherously	

Adjectives used as adverbs

Certain adjectives are used adverbially. These include: **bas, bon, cher, clair, court, doux, droit, dur, faux, ferme, fort, haut, mauvais** and **net** (→**11**)

1 *MASC./FEM. ADJECTIVE* — *ADVERB*

heureux/heureuse fortunate	**heureusement** fortunately
franc/franche frank	**franchement** frankly
extrême/extrême extreme	**extrêmement** extremely

2 *MASC. ADJECTIVE* — *ADVERB*

désespéré desperate	**désespérément** desperately
vrai true	**vraiment** truly
résolu resolute	**résolument** resolutely

3 **gai** cheerful — **gaiement** OR **gaîment** cheerfully

4 **continu** continuous — **continûment** continuously

5

constant constant	**constamment** constantly
courant fluent	**couramment** fluently
évident obvious	**évidemment** obviously
fréquent frequent	**fréquemment** frequently

6

lent slow	**lentement** slowly
présent present	**présentement** presently

7 **Elle travaille bien**
She works well

8 **Il a expressément défendu qu'on parte**
He has expressly forbidden us to leave

9 **Un emploi mal payé**
A badly paid job

10 **J'ai été profondément ému**
I was deeply moved

11 **parler bas/haut**
to speak softly/loudly
coûter cher
to be expensive
voir clair
to see clearly
travailler dur
to work hard
chanter faux
to sing off key
sentir bon/mauvais
to smell nice/horrible

Position of Adverbs

● When the adverb accompanies a verb in a simple tense, it generally follows the verb (→ 1)
● When the adverb accompanies a verb in a compound tense, it generally comes between the auxiliary verb and the past participle (→ 2)
  Some adverbs, however, follow the past participle (→ 3)
● When the adverb accompanies an adjective or another adverb it generally precedes the adjective/adverb (→ 4)

Comparatives of Adverbs

These are formed using the following constructions:

plus ... (que)	more ... (than)	(→ 5)
moins ... (que)	less ... (than)	(→ 6)
aussi ... que	as ... as	(→ 7)
si ... que*	as ... as	(→ 8)

*used mainly after a negative

Superlatives of Adverbs

These are formed using the following constructions:

le plus ... (que)	the most ... (that)	(→ 9)
le moins ... (que)	the least ... (that)	(→ 10)

Adverbs with irregular comparatives/superlatives

ADVERB	COMPARATIVE	SUPERLATIVE
beaucoup	**plus**	**le plus**
a lot	*more*	*(the) most*
bien	**mieux**	**le mieux**
well	*better*	*(the) best*
mal	**pis** OR	**le pis** OR
	plus mal	**le plus mal**
badly	*worse*	*(the) worst*
peu	**moins**	**le moins**
little	*less*	*(the) least*

1 **Il dort encore**   **Je pense souvent à toi**
He's still asleep   I often think about you

2 **Ils sont déjà partis**   **J'ai toujours cru que ...**
They've already gone   I've always thought that ...
J'ai presque fini   **Il a trop mangé**
I'm almost finished   He's eaten too much

3 **On les a vus partout**   **Elle est revenue hier**
We saw them everywhere   She came back yesterday

4 **un très beau chemisier**   **une femme bien habillée**
a very nice blouse   a well-dressed woman
beaucoup plus vite   **peu souvent**
much faster   not very often

5 **plus vite**   **plus régulièrement**
more quickly   more regularly
Elle chante plus fort que moi
She sings louder than I do

6 **moins facilement**   **moins souvent**
less easily   less often
Nous nous voyons moins fréquemment qu'auparavant
We see each other less frequently than before

7 **Faites-le aussi vite que possible**
Do it as quickly as possible
Il en sait aussi long que nous
He knows as much about it as we do

8 **Ce n'est pas si loin que je pensais**
It's not as far as I thought

9 **Marianne court le plus vite**
Marianne runs fastest
Le plus tôt que je puisse venir c'est samedi
The earliest that I can come is Saturday

10 **C'est l'auteur que je connais le moins bien**
It's the writer I'm least familiar with

Common adverbs and their usage

assez	*enough; quite*	(→ 1) See also below
aussi	*also, too; as*	(→ 2)
autant	*as much*	(→ 3) See also below
beaucoup	*a lot; much*	(→ 4) See also below
bien	*well; very*	(→ 5) See also below
	very much; 'indeed'	
combien	*how much; how many*	(→ 6) See also below
comme	*how; what*	(→ 7)
déjà	*already; before*	(→ 8)
encore	*still; yet*	(→ 9)
	more; even	
moins	*less*	(→ 10) See also below
peu	*little, not much; not very*	(→ 11) See also below
plus	*more*	(→ 12) See also below
si	*so; such*	(→ 13)
tant	*so much*	(→ 14) See also below
toujours	*always; still*	(→ 15)
trop	*too much; too*	(→ 16) See also below

● **assez, autant, beaucoup, combien** etc. are used in the construction *adverb* + **de** + *noun* with the following meanings:

assez de	*enough*	(→17)
autant de	*as much; as many*	
	so much; so many	
beaucoup de	*a lot of*	
combien de	*how much; how many*	
moins de	*less; fewer*	(→17)
peu de	*little, not much; few,*	
	not many	
plus de	*more*	
tant de	*so much; so many*	
trop de	*too much; too many*	

● **bien** can be followed by a partitive article (see p. 144) plus a noun to mean *a lot of; a good many* (→ 18)

1 **Avez-vous assez chaud?**
Are you warm enough?

Il est assez tard
It's quite late

2 **Je préfère ça aussi**
I prefer it too

Elle est aussi grande que moi
She is as tall as I am

3 **Je voyage autant que lui**
I have as much as him

C'est beaucoup plus loin?
Is it much further?

4 **Tu lis beaucoup?**
Do you read a lot?

Je suis bien content que ...
I'm very pleased that ...

5 **Bien joué!**
Well played!

Il s'est bien amusé
He enjoyed himself very much

Je l'ai bien fait
I DID do it

6 **Combien coûte ce livre?**
How much is this book?

Vous êtes combien?
How many of you are there?

7 **Comme tu es jolie!**
How pretty you look!

Comme il fait beau!
What lovely weather!

8 **Je l'ai déjà fait**
I've already done it

Êtes-vous déjà allé en France?
Have you been to France before?

9 **J'en ai encore deux**
I've still got two

Elle n'est pas encore là
She isn't there yet

Encore du café, Alain?
More coffee, Alain?

Encore mieux!
Even better!

10 **Travaillez moins**
Work less

Je suis moins étonné que toi
I'm less surprised than you are

11 **Elle mange peu**
She doesn't eat very much

C'est peu important
It's not very important

12 **Il se détend plus**
He relaxes more

Elle est plus timide que Sophie
She is shyer than Sophie

13 **Simon est si charmant**
Simon is so charming

une si belle vue
such a lovely view

14 **Elle l'aime tant** She loves him so much

15 **Il dit toujours ça!**
He always says that!

Tu le vois toujours?
Do you still see him?

16 **J'ai trop mangé**
I've eaten too much

C'est trop cher
It's too expensive

17 **assez d'argent / de livres**
enough money/books

moins de temps / d'amis
less time/fewer friends

18 **bien du mal / des gens** a lot of harm/a good many people

On the following pages you will find some of the most frequent uses of prepositions in French. Particular attention is paid to cases where usage differs markedly from English. It is often difficult to give an English equivalent for French prepositions, since usage *does* vary so much between the two languages.

In the list below, the broad meaning of the preposition is given on the left, with examples of usage following.

Prepositions are dealt with in alphabetical order, except **à**, **de** and **en** which are shown first.

à

at	**lancer qch à qn**	*to throw sth at sb*
	il habite à St. Pierre	*he lives at St. Pierre*
	à 5 francs (la) pièce	*(at) 5 francs each*
	à 100 km à l'heure	*at 100 km per hour*
in	**à la campagne**	*in the country*
	à Londres	*in London*
	au lit	*in bed (also to bed)*
	un livre à la main	*with a book in his/her hand*
on	**un tableau au mur**	*a picture on the wall*
to	**aller au cinéma**	*to go to the cinema*
	donner qch à qn	*to give sth to sb*
	le premier/dernier à faire	*the first/last to do*
	demander qch à qn	*to ask sb sth*
from	**arracher qch à qn**	*to snatch sth from sb*
	acheter qch à qn	*to buy sth from sb*
	cacher qch à qn	*to hide sth from sb*
	emprunter qch à qn	*to borrow sth from sb*
	prendre qch à qn	*to take sth from sb*
	voler qch à qn	*to steal sth from sb*

descriptive	**la femme au chapeau vert**	*the woman with the green hat*
	un garçon aux yeux bleus	*a boy with blue eyes*
manner, means	**à l'anglaise**	*in the English manner*
	fait à la main	*handmade*
	à bicyclette/cheval	*by bicycle/on horseback (BUT note other forms of transport used with **en** and **par**)*
	à pied	*on foot*
	chauffer au gaz	*to heat with/by gas*
	à pas lents	*with slow steps*
	cuisiner au beurre	*to cook with butter*
time, date: *at, in*	**à minuit**	*at midnight*
	à trois heures cinq	*at five past three*
	au 20ème siècle	*in the 20th century*
	à Noël/Pâques	*at Christmas/Easter*
distance	**à 6 km d'ici**	*(at a distance of) 6 km from here*
	à deux pas de chez moi	*just a step from my place*
destined for	**une tasse à thé**	*a teacup (compare **une tasse de thé**)*
	un service à café	*a coffee service*
after certain adjectives	**son écriture est difficile à lire**	*his writing is difficult to read (compare the usage with **de**, p. 206)*
	prêt à tout	*ready for anything*
after certain verbs *Continued*	see p. 64	

de

from	**venir de Londres**	*to come from London*
	du matin au soir	*from morning till night*
	du 21 juin au 5 juillet	*from 21st June till 5th July*
	de 10 à 15	*from 10 to 15*
belonging to, *of*	**un ami de la famille**	*a family friend*
	les vents d'automne	*the autumn winds*
contents, composition, material	**une boîte d'allumettes**	*a box of matches*
	une tasse de thé	*a cup of tea* (compare **une tasse à thé**)
	une robe de soie	*a silk dress*
manner	**d'une façon irrégulière**	*in an irregular way*
	d'un coup de couteau	*with the blow of a knife*
quality	**la société de consommation**	*the consumer society*
	des objets de valeur	*valuable items*
comparative + a number	**il y avait plus/moins de cent personnes**	*there were more/fewer than a hundred people*
after superlatives: *in*	**la plus/moins belle ville du monde**	*the most/least beautiful city in the world*
after certain adjectives	**surpris de voir**	*surprised to see*
	il est difficile d'y accéder	*access is difficult* (compare the usage with **à**, p. 205)
after certain verbs	see p. 64	

en

place: *to, in, on*	en ville	*in/to town*
	en pleine mer	*on the open sea*
	en France	*in/to France* (note that masculine countries use **à**)
dates, months: *in*	en 1923	*in 1923*
	en janvier	*in January*
transport	en voiture	*by car*
	en avion	*by plane* (but note usage of **à** and **par** in other expressions)
language	en français	*in French*
duration	je le ferai en trois jours	*I'll do it in three days* (i.e. *I'll take 3 days to do it*: compare **dans trois jours**)
material	un bracelet en or	*a bracelet made of gold* (note that the use of **en** stresses the material more than the use of **de**)
	consister en	*to consist of*
in the manner of, like a	parler en vrai connaisseur	*to speak like a real connoisseur*
	déguisé en cowboy	*dressed up as a cowboy*
+ present participle	il l'a vu en passant devant la porte	*he saw it as he came past the door*

Continued

avant

before	**il est arrivé avant toi**	*he arrived before you*
+ infinitive (add **de**)	**je vais finir ça avant de manger**	*I'm going to finish this before eating*
preference	**la santé avant tout**	*health above all things*

chez

at the home of	**chez lui/moi**	*at his/my house*
	être chez soi	*to be at home*
	venez chez nous	*come round to our place*
at/to a shop	**chez le boucher**	*at/to the butcher's*
in a person, *among* a group of people or animals	**ce que je n'aime pas chez lui c'est son ...**	*what I don't like in him is his ...*
	chez les fourmis	*among ants*

dans

position	**dans une boîte**	*in(to) a box*
circumstance	**dans son enfance**	*in his childhood*
future time	**dans trois jours**	*in three days' time (compare **en trois jours**, p. 207)*

depuis

since: time place	**depuis mardi**	*since Tuesday*
	il pleut depuis Paris	*it's been raining since Paris*
for	**il habite cette maison depuis 3 ans**	*he's been living in this house for 3 years (NOTE TENSE)*

dès

past time	**dès mon enfance**	*since my childhood*
future time	**je le ferai dès mon retour**	*I'll do it as soon as I get back*

entre

between	**entre 8 et 10**	*between 8 and 10*
among	**Jean et Pierre, entre autres**	*Jean and Pierre, among others*
reciprocal	**s'aider entre eux**	*to help each other (out)*

d'entre

of, among	**trois d'entre eux**	*three of them*

par

agent of passive: *by*	**renversé par une voiture**	*knocked down by a car*
	tué par la foudre	*killed by lightning*
weather conditions	**par un beau jour d'été**	*on a lovely summer's day*
by (means of)	**par un couloir/sentier**	*by a corridor/path*
	par le train	*by train (but see also* **à** *and* **en***)*
	par l'intermédiaire de M. Duval	*through Mr. Duval*
distribution	**deux par deux**	*two by two*
	par groupes de dix	*in groups of ten*
	deux fois par jour	*twice a day*

Continued

pour

for	c'est pour vous	it's for you
	c'est pour demain	it's for tomorrow
	une chambre pour 2 nuits	a room for 2 nights
	pour un enfant, il se débrouille bien	for a child he manages very well
	il part pour l'Espagne	he's leaving for Spain
	il l'a fait pour vous	he did it for you
	il lui a donné 50 francs pour ce livre	he gave him 50 francs for this book
	je ne suis pas pour cette idée	I'm not for that idea
	pour qui me prends-tu?	who do you take me for?
	il passe pour un idiot	he's taken for a fool
+ infinitive: (in order) to	elle se pencha pour le ramasser	she bent down to pick it up
	c'est trop fragile pour servir de siège	it's too fragile to be used as a seat
to(wards)	être bon/gentil pour qn	to be kind to sb
with prices, time	pour 200 francs d'essence	200 francs' worth of petrol
	j'en ai encore pour une heure	I'll be another hour (at it) yet

sans

without	sans eau	without water
	sans ma femme	without my wife
+ infinitive	sans compter les autres	without counting the others

sauf

except (for)	**tous sauf lui**	*all except him*
	sauf quand il pleut	*except when its raining*
barring	**sauf imprévu**	*barring the unexpected*
	sauf avis contraire	*unless you hear to the contrary*

sur

on	**sur le siège**	*on the seat*
	sur l'armoire	*on top of the wardrobe*
	sur le mur	*on (top of) the wall (if the meaning is hanging on the wall use à, p. 204)*
	sur votre gauche	*on your left*
	être sur le point de faire	*to be on the point of doing*
on (to)	**mettez-le sur la table**	*put it on the table*
proportion: out of; by	**8 sur 10**	*8 out of 10*
	un automobiliste sur 5	*one motorist in 5*
	la pièce fait 2 mètres sur 3	*the room measures 2 metres by 3*

Conjunctions

There are conjunctions which introduce a main clause, such as **et** *and*, **mais** *but*, **si** *if*, **ou** *or* etc., and those which introduce subordinate clauses like **parce que** *because*, **pendant que** *while*, **après que** *after* etc. They are all used in much the same way as in English, but the following points are of note:

- Some conjunctions in French require a following subjunctive, see p. 58

- Some conjunctions are 'split' in French like *both...and, either... or* in English:

et...et	*both...and*	(→ **1**)
ni...ni...ne	*neither...nor*	(→ **2**)
ou (bien) .. ou (bien)	*either...or (else)*	(→ **3**)
soit...soit	*either...or*	(→ **4**)

- **si + il(s) → s'il(s)** (→ **5**)

- **que**
  - meaning *that* (→ **6**)
  - replacing another conjunction (→ **7**)
  - replacing **si**, see p. 62
  - in comparisons, meaning *as, than* (→ **8**)
  - followed by the subjunctive, see p. 62

- **aussi** *so, therefore*: the subject and verb are inverted if the subject is a pronoun (→ **9**)

1 Ces fleurs poussent et en été et en hiver
These flowers grow in both summer and winter

2 Ni lui ni elle ne sont venus
Neither he nor she came
Ils n'ont ni argent ni nourriture
They have neither money nor food

3 Elle doit être ou naïve ou stupide
She must be either naïve or stupid
Ou bien il m'évite ou bien il ne me reconnaît pas
Either he's avoiding me or else he doesn't recognise me

4 Il faut choisir soit l'un soit l'autre
You have to choose either one or the other

5 Je ne sais pas s'il vient/s'ils viennent
I don't know if he's coming/if they're coming
Dis-moi s'il y a des erreurs
Tell me if there are any mistakes
Votre passeport, s'il vous plaît
Your passport, please

6 Il dit qu'il t'a vu
He says (that) he saw you
Est-ce qu'elle sait que vous êtes là?
Does she know that you're here?

7 Quand tu seras plus grand et que tu auras une maison à toi, ...
When you're older and you have a house of your own, ...
Comme il pleuvait et que je n'avais pas de parapluie, ...
As it was raining and I didn't have an umbrella, ...

8 Ils n'y vont pas aussi souvent que nous
They don't go there as often as we do
Il les aime plus que jamais
He likes them more than ever
L'argent est moins lourd que le plomb
Silver is lighter than lead

9 Ceux-ci sont plus rares, aussi coûtent-ils cher
These ones are rarer, so they're expensive

Word Order

Word order in French is largely the same as in English, except for the following. Most of these have already been dealt with under the appropriate part of speech, but are summarised here along with other instances not covered elsewhere.

- Object pronouns nearly always come before the verb (→ **1**)
  For details, see pp. 166 to 170

- Certain adjectives come after the noun (→ **2**)
  For details, see p. 162

- Adverbs accompanying a verb in a simple tense usually follow the verb (→ **3**)
  For details, see p. 200

- After **aussi** *so, therefore*, **à peine** *hardly*, **peut-être** *perhaps*, the verb and subject are inverted (→ **4**)

- After the relative pronoun **dont** *whose* (→ **5**)
  For details, see p. 182

- In exclamations, **que** and **comme** do not affect the normal word order (→ **6**)

- Following direct speech:
  - the *verb* + *subject* order is inverted to become *subject* + *verb* (→ **7**)
  - with a pronoun subject, the verb and pronoun are linked by a hyphen (→ **8**)
  - when the verb ends in a vowel in the 3rd person singular, **-t-** is inserted between the pronoun and the verb (→ **9**)

For word order in negative sentences, see p. 216
For word order in interrogative sentences, see pp. 220 and 222

1 Je les vois!
   I can see them!

   Il me l'a donné
   He gave it to me

2 une ville française
   a French town

   du vin rouge
   some red wine

3 Il pleut encore
   It's still raining

   Elle m'aide quelquefois
   She sometimes helps me

4 Il vit tout seul, aussi fait-il ce qu'il veut
   He lives alone, so he does what he likes

   A peine la pendule avait-elle sonné trois heures que ...
   Hardly had the clock struck three when ...

   Peut-être avez-vous raison
   Perhaps you're right

5 Compare: **un homme dont je connais la fille**
                a man whose daughter I know

   and: **un homme dont la fille me connaît**
          a man whose daughter knows me

   If the person (or object) 'owned' is the *object* of the verb, the order
   is:
   dont + verb + noun (1st sentence)
   If the person (or object) 'owned' is the *subject* of the verb, the order
   is:
   dont + noun + verb (2nd sentence)

   Note also: **l'homme dont elle est la fille**
                the man whose daughter she is

6 Qu'il fait chaud!
   How warm it is!

   Que je suis content de vous voir!
   How pleased I am to see you!

   Comme c'est cher
   How expensive it is!

   Que tes voisins sont gentils!
   How kind your neighbours are!

7 'Je pense que oui' a dit Luc
   'I think so,' said Luke

   'Ça ne fait rien' répondit Jean
   'It doesn't matter,' John replied

8 'Quelle horreur!' me suis-je exclamé
   'How awful!' I exclaimed

9 'Pourquoi pas?' a-t-elle demandé
   'Why not?' she asked

   'Si c'est vrai,' continua-t-il '...'
   'If it's true,' he went on '...'

Negatives

ne ... pas	not
ne ... point (literary)	not
ne ... rien	nothing
ne ... personne	nobody
ne ... plus	no longer, no more
ne ... jamais	never
ne ... que	only
ne ... aucun(e)	no
ne ... nul(le)	no
ne ... nulle part	nowhere
ne ... ni	neither ... nor
ne ... ni ... ni	neither ... nor

● **Word order**

– In simple tenses and the imperative:
  ne precedes the verb (and any object pronouns) and the second
  element follows the verb (→ **1**)

– In compound tenses:
  i **ne ... pas, ne ... point, ne ... rien, ne ... plus, ne ...
    jamais, ne ... guère** follow the pattern:
    ne + auxiliary verb + **pas** + past participle (→ **2**)
  ii **ne ... personne, ne ... que, ne ... aucun(e), ne ... nul(le),
    ne ... nulle part, ne ... ni (... ni)** follow the pattern:
    ne + auxiliary verb + past participle + **personne** (→ **3**)

– With a verb in the infinitive:
  ne ... pas, ne ... point (etc. see i above) come together (→ **4**)

● For use of **rien**, **personne** and **aucun** as pronouns, see p. 178

Continued

1 Je ne fume pas
I don't smoke
Ne changez rien
Don't change anything
Je ne vois personne
I can't see anybody
Nous ne nous verrons plus
We won't see each other any more
Il n'arrive jamais à l'heure
He never arrives on time
Il n'avait qu'une valise
He only had one suitcase
Je n'ai reçu aucune réponse
I have received no reply
Il ne boit ni ne fume
He neither drinks nor smokes
Ni mon fils ni ma fille ne les connaissaient
Neither my son nor my daughter knew them

2 Elle n'a pas fait ses devoirs
She hasn't done her homework
Ne vous a-t-il rien dit?
Didn't he say anything to you?
Ils n'avaient jamais vu une si belle maison
They had never seen such a beautiful house
Tu n'as guère changé
You've hardly changed

3 Je n'ai parlé à personne
I haven't spoken to anybody
Il n'avait mangé que la moitié du repas
He had only eaten half the meal
Elle ne les a trouvés nulle part
She couldn't find them anywhere
Il ne l'avait ni vu ni entendu
He had neither seen nor heard him

4 Il essayait de ne pas rire
He was trying not to laugh

Negatives (ctd.)

- Combination of negatives.
  These are the most common combinations of negative particles:

ne ... plus jamais	(→ 1)
ne ... plus personne	(→ 2)
ne ... plus rien	(→ 3)
ne ... plus ni ... ni ...	(→ 4)
ne ... jamais personne	(→ 5)
ne ... jamais rien	(→ 6)
ne ... jamais que	(→ 7)
ne ... jamais ni ... ni ...	(→ 8)
(ne ... pas) non plus	(→ 9)

non and pas

- **non** *no* is the usual negative response to a question (→ 10)
  It is often translated as *not* (→ 11)
- **pas** is generally used when a distinction is being made, or for emphasis (→ 12)
  It is often translated as *not* (→ 13)

1 **Je ne le ferai plus jamais**
I'll never do it again

2 **Je ne connais plus personne à Rouen**
I don't know anybody in Rouen any more

3 **Ces marchandises ne valaient plus rien**
Those goods were no longer worth anything

4 **Ils n'ont plus ni chats ni chiens**
They no longer have either cats or dogs

5 **On n'y voit jamais personne**
You never see anybody there

6 **Ils ne font jamais rien d'intéressant**
They never do anything interesting

7 **Je n'ai jamais parlé qu'à sa femme**
I've only ever spoken to his wife

8 **Il ne m'a jamais ni écrit ni téléphoné**
He has never either written to me or phoned me

9 **Ils n'ont pas d'enfants et nous non plus**
They don't have any children and neither do we
Je ne les aime pas – Moi non plus
I don't like them – Neither do I; I don't either

10 **Vous voulez nous accompagner? – Non**
Do you want to come with us? – No (I don't)

11 **Tu viens ou non?**
Are you coming or not?
J'espère que non
I hope not

12 **Ma sœur aime le ski, moi pas**
My sister likes skiing, I don't

13 **Qui a fait ça? – Pas moi!**
Who did that? – Not me!
Est-il de retour? – Pas encore
Is he back? – Not yet
Tu as froid? – Pas du tout
Are you cold? – Not at all

Question forms: direct

There are four ways of forming direct questions in French:

- by inverting the normal word order so that
  pronoun subject + verb → verb + pronoun subject.
  A hyphen links the verb and pronoun (→ **1**)

  – When the subject is a noun, a pronoun is inserted after the verb
    and linked to it by a hyphen (→ **2**)

  – When the verb ends in a vowel in the third person singular, **-t-** is
    inserted before the pronoun (→ **3**)

- by maintaining the word order *subject + verb*, but by using a rising
  intonation at the end of the sentence (→ **4**)

- by inserting **est-ce que** before the construction *subject + verb* (→ **5**)

- by using an interrogative word at the beginning of the sentence,
  together with inversion *or* the **est-ce que** form above (→ **6**)

1 Aimez-vous la France?
   Do you like France?
   Est-ce possible?
   Is it possible?
   Part-on tout de suite?
   Are we leaving right away?

   Avez-vous fini?
   Have you finished?
   Est-elle restée?
   Did she stay?

2 Tes parents sont-ils en vacances?
   Are your parents on holiday?
   Jean-Benoît est-il parti?
   Has Jean-Benoît left?

3 A-t-elle de l'argent?
   Has she any money?
   La pièce dure-t-elle longtemps?
   Does the play last long?
   Mon père a-t-il téléphoné?
   Has my father phoned?

4 Il l'a fini
   He's finished it
   Robert va venir
   Robert's coming

   Il l'a fini?
   Has he finished it?
   Robert va venir?
   Is Robert coming?

5 Est-ce que tu la connais?
   Do you know her?
   Est-ce que tes parents sont revenus d'Italie?
   Have your parents come back from Italy?

6 Quel train { **prends-tu?**
                  { **est-ce que tu prends?**
   What train are you getting?
   Lequel { **est-ce que ta sœur préfère?**
             { **ta sœur préfère-t-elle?**
   Which one does your sister prefer?
   Quand { **êtes-vous arrivé?**
            { **est-ce que vous êtes arrivé?**
   When did you arrive?
   Pourquoi { **ne sont-ils pas venus?**
               { **est-ce qu'ils ne sont pas venus?**
   Why haven't they come?

Question forms: indirect

An indirect question is one that is 'reported', e.g. he asked me *what the time was*, tell me *which way to go*. Word order in indirect questions is as follows:

- *interrogative word* + *subject* + *verb* (→ **1**)

- when the subject is a noun, and not a pronoun, the subject and verb are often inverted (→ **2**)

n'est-ce pas

This is used wherever English would use *isn't it?*, *don't they?*, *weren't we?*, *is it?* etc. tagged on to the end of a sentence (→ **3**)

oui and si

Oui is the word for *yes* in answer to a question put in the affirmative (→ **4**)
Si is the word for *yes* in answer to a question put in the negative or to contradict a negative statement (→ **5**)

1 Je me demande s'il viendra
   I wonder if he'll come
   Je ne sais pas à quoi ça sert
   I don't know what it's for
   Dites-moi quel autobus va à la gare
   Tell me which bus goes to the station
   Il m'a demandé combien d'argent j'avais
   He asked me how much money I had

2 Elle ne sait pas à quelle heure commence le film
   She doesn't know what time the film starts
   Je me demande où sont mes clés
   I wonder where my keys are
   Elle nous a demandé comment allait notre père
   She asked us how our father was
   je ne sais pas ce que veulent dire ces mots
   I don't know what these words mean

3 Il fait chaud, n'est-ce pas?
   It's warm, isn't it?
   Vous n'oublierez pas, n'est-ce pas?
   You won't forget, will you?

4 Tu l'as fait? – Oui
   Have you done it? – Yes (I have)

5 Tu ne l'as pas fait? – Si
   Haven't you done it? – Yes (I have)

Numbers

Cardinal (*one, two etc.*)		Ordinal (*first, second etc.*)	
zéro	0		
un (une)	1	premier (première)	1er, 1ère
deux	2	deuxième, second(e)	2ème
trois	3	troisième	3ème
quatre	4	quatrième	4ème
cinq	5	cinquième	5ème
six	6	sixième	6ème
sept	7	septième	7ème
huit	8	huitième	8ème
neuf	9	neuvième	9ème
dix	10	dixième	10ème
onze	11	onzième	11ème
douze	12	douzième	12ème
treize	13	treizième	13ème
quatorze	14	quatorzième	14ème
quinze	15	quinzième	15ème
seize	16	seizième	16ème
dix-sept	17	dix-septième	17ème
dix-huit	18	dix-huitième	18ème
dix-neuf	19	dix-neuvième	19ème
vingt	20	vingtième	20ème
vingt et un (une)	21	vingt et unième	21ème
vingt-deux	22	vingt-deuxième	22ème
vingt-trois	23	vingt-troisième	23ème
trente	30	trentième	30ème
quarante	40	quarantième	40ème
cinquante	50	cinquantième	50ème
soixante	60	soixantième	60ème
soixante-dix	70	soixante-dixième	70ème
soixante et onze	71	soixante-onzième	71ème
soixante-douze	72	soixante-douzième	72ème
quatre-vingts	80	quatre-vingtième	80ème
quatre-vingt-un (une)	81	quatre-vingt-unième	81ème
quatre-vingt-dix	90	quatre-vingt-dixième	90ème
quatre-vingt-onze	91	quatre-vingt-onzième	91ème

Numbers (ctd.)

Cardinal		Ordinal	
cent	100	centième	100ème
cent un (une)	101	cent unième	101ème
cent deux	102	cent deuxième	102ème
cent dix	110	cent dixième	110ème
cent quarante-deux	142	cent quarante-deuxième	142ème
deux cents	200	deux centième	200ème
duex cent un (une)	201	deux cent unième	201ème
duex cent deux	202	deux cent-deuxième	202ème
trois cents	300	trois centième	300ème
quatre cents	400	quatre centième	400ème
cinq cents	500	cinq centième	500ème
six cents	600	six centième	600ème
sept cents	700	sept centième	700ème
huit cents	800	huit centième	800ème
neuf cents	900	neuf centième	900ème
mille	1000	millième	1000ème
mille un (une)	1001	mille unième	1001ème
mille deux	1002	mille deuxième	1002ème
deux mille	2000	deux millième	2000ème
cent mille	100.000	cent millième	100.000ème
un million	1.000.000	millionième	1.000.000ème
deux millions	2.000.000	deux millionième	2.000.000ème

Fractions		Others	
un demi, une demie	½	zéro virgule cinq	0,5
un tiers	⅓	un virgule trois	1,3
deux tiers	⅔	dix pour cent	10%
un quart	¼	deux plus deux	2 + 2
trois quarts	¾	deux moins deux	2 – 2
un cinquième	⅕	deux fois deux	2 × 2
cinq et trois quarts	5¾	deux divisé par deux	2 ÷ 2

Note the use of points with large numbers and commas with fractions,
i.e. the opposite of English usage.

Numbers: Other Uses

- **-aine** denoting approximate numbers:

une douzaine (de pommes)	about a dozen (apples)
une quinzaine (d'hommes)	about fifteen (men)
des centaines de personnes	hundreds of people
BUT: **un millier (de voitures)**	about a thousand (cars)

- measurements:

vingt mètres carrés	20 square metres
vingt mètres cubes	20 cubic metres
un pont long de quarante mètres	a bridge 40 metres long
avoir trois mètres de large/de haut	to be 3 metres wide/high

- miscellaneous:

Il habite au dix	He lives at number 10
C'est au chapitre sept	It's in chapter 7
(C'est) à la page 17	(It's) on page 17
(Il habite) au septième étage	(He lives) on the 7th floor
Il est arrivé le septième	He came in 7th
échelle au vingt-cinq millième	scale 1:25,000

Telephone numbers

Je voudrais Edimbourg trois cent trente, vingt-deux, dix
I would like Edinburgh 330 22 10

Je voudrais le soixante-cinq, treize, vingt-deux, zéro deux
Could you get me 65 13 22 02

Poste trois cent trente-cinq
Extension number 335

Poste vingt-deux, trente-trois
Extension number 22 33

N.B. In French, telephone numbers are broken down into groups of two or three numbers (never four), and are not spoken separately as in English. They are also written in groups of two or three numbers.

The calendar

Dates

Quelle est la date d'aujourd'hui?
Quel jour sommes-nous? } What's the date today?

C'est ...
Nous sommes ... } It's the ...

le premier février	1st of February
le deux février	2nd of February
le vingt-huit février	28th of February

Il vient le sept mars   He's coming on the 7th of March

N.B. Use cardinal numbers except for the first of the month.

Years

Je suis né en 1971
I was born in 1971

le douze février { **dix-neuf cent soixante et onze**
                  { **mil neuf cent soixante et onze**
(on) 12th February 1971

N.B. There are two ways of expressing the year (see last example).
Note the spelling of **mil** *one thousand* in dates.

Other expressions

dans les années cinquante	during the fifties
au vingtième siècle	in the twentieth century
en mai	in May
lundi (quinze)	on Monday (the 15th)
le lundi	on Mondays
dans dix jours	in 10 days' time
il y a dix jours	10 days ago

The Time

Quelle heure est-il?	*What time is it?*
Il est ...	*It's ...*

00.00	**minuit** *midnight, twelve o'clock*
00.10	**minuit dix, zéro heure dix**
00.15	**minuit et quart, zéro heure quinze**
00.30	**minuit et demi, zéro heure trente**
00.45	**une heure moins (le) quart, zéro heure quarante-cinq**
01.00	**une heure du matin** *one a.m., one o'clock in the morning*
01.10	**une heure dix (du matin)**
01.15	**une heure et quart, une heure quinze**
01.30	**une heure et demie, une heure trente**
01.45	**deux heures moins (le) quart, une heure quarante-cinq**
01.50	**deux heures moins dix, une heure cinquante**
01.59	**deux heures moins une, une heure cinquante-neuf**
12.00	**midi, douze heures** *noon, twelve o'clock*
12.30	**midi et demi, douze heures trente**
13.00	**une heure de l'après-midi, treize heures** *one p.m., one o'clock in the afternoon*
01.30	**une heure et demie (de l'après-midi), treize heures trente**
19.00	**sept heures du soir, dix-neuf heures** *seven p.m., seven o'clock in the evening*
19.30	**sept heures et demie (du soir), dix-neuf heures trente**

A quelle heure venez-vous? – A sept heures
What time are you coming? – At seven o'clock
Les bureaux sont fermés de midi à quatorze heures
The offices are closed from twelve until two
à deux heures du matin/de l'après-midi
at two o'clock in the morning/afternoon, at two a.m./p.m.
à sept heures du soir
at seven o'clock in the evening, at seven p.m.
à cinq heures précises *or* **pile**
at five o'clock sharp
vers neuf heures
about nine o'clock
peu avant/après midi
shortly before/after noon
entre huit et neuf heures
between eight and nine o'clock
Il est plus de trois heures et demie
It's after half past three
Il faut y être à dix heures au plus tard/au plus tôt
You have to be there by ten o'clock at the latest/earliest
Ne venez pas plus tard que onze heures moins le quart
Come no later than a quarter to eleven
Il en a pour une demi-heure
He'll be half an hour (at it)
Elle est restée sans connaissance pendant un quart d'heure
She was unconscious for a quarter of an hour
Je les attends depuis une heure
I've been waiting for them for an hour/since one o'clock
Ils sont partis il y a quelques minutes
They left a few minutes ago
Je l'ai fait en vingt minutes
I did it in twenty minutes
Le train arrive dans une heure
The train arrives in an hour('s time)
Combien de temps dure ce film?
How long does this film last?

Beware of translating word for word. While on occasion this is quite possible, quite often it is not. The need for caution is illustrated by the following:

● English phrasal verbs (i.e. verbs followed by a preposition) e.g. *to run away*, *to fall down* are often translated by one word in French (→ **1**)

● English verbal constructions often contain a preposition where none exists in French, or vice versa (→ **2**)

● Two or more prepositions in English may have a single rendering in French (→ **3**)

● A word which is singular in English may be plural in French, or vice versa (→ **4**)

● French has no equivalent of the possessive construction denoted by --'s/--'s (→ **5**)
See also *at/in/to*, p. 234

Specific problems

-ing

This is translated in a variety of ways in French:

● *to be ...-ing* is translated by a simple verb (→ **6**)
Exception: when a physical position is denoted, a past participle is used (→ **7**)

● in the construction *to see/hear sb ...-ing*, use an infinitive or **qui** + verb (→ **8**)

-ing can also be translated by:
  – an infinitive (→ **9**)
    (see p. 44)
  – a perfect infinitive (→ **10**)
    (see p. 46)
  – a present participle (→ **11**)
    (see p. 48)
  – a noun (→ **12**)

Continued

1 s'enfuir
to run away

tomber
to fall down

céder
to give in

2 payer
to pay for

regarder
to look at

écouter
to listen to

obéir à
to obey

nuire à
to harm

manquer de
to lack

3 s'étonner de
to be surprised at

satisfait de
satisfied with

voler qch à
to steal sth from

apte à
capable of; fit for

4 les bagages
the luggage

ses cheveux
his/her hair

le bétail
the cattle

mon pantalon
my trousers

5 la voiture de mon frère
my brother's car
(literally: ... of my brother)

la chambre des enfants
the children's bedroom
(literally: ... of the children)

6 Il part demain
He's leaving tomorrow

Je lisais un roman
I was reading a novel

7 Elle est assise là-bas
She's sitting over there

Il était couché par terre
He was lying on the ground

8 Je les vois $\left\{ \begin{array}{l} \text{venir} \\ \text{qui viennent} \end{array} \right\}$ I can see them coming

Je l'ai entendue $\left\{ \begin{array}{l} \text{chanter} \\ \text{qui chantait} \end{array} \right\}$ I heard her singing

9 J'aime aller au cinéma
I like going to the cinema

Arrêtez de parler!
Stop talking!

Au lieu de répondre
Instead of answering

Avant de partir
Before leaving

10 Après avoir ouvert la boîte, il ...
After opening the box, he ...

11 Etant plus timide que moi, elle ...
Being shyer than me, she ...

12 Le ski me maintient en forme
Skiing keeps me fit

to be

- Generally translated by **être** (→ 1)
  When physical location is implied, **se trouver** may be used (→ 2)

- In set expressions, describing physical and emotional conditions, **avoir** is used:

avoir chaud/froid	*to be warm/cold*
avoir faim/soif	*to be hungry/thirsty*
avoir peur/honte	*to be afraid/ashamed*
avoir tort/raison	*to be wrong/right*

- Describing the weather, e.g. *what's the weather like?, it's windy/sunny*, use **faire** (→ 3)

- For ages, e.g. *he is 6*, use **avoir** (→ 4)

- For state of health, e.g. *he's unwell, how are you?*, use **aller** (→ 5)

it is, it's

- Usually **il/elle est**, when referring to a noun (→ 6)

- For expressions of time, also use **il est** (→ 7)

- To describe the weather, e.g. *it's windy*, see above

- In the construction: *it is difficult/easy to do sth*, use **il est** (→ 8)

- In all other constructions, use **c'est** (→ 9)

there is/there are

- Both are translated by **il y a** (→ 10)

can, be able

- Physical ability is expressed by **pouvoir** (→ 11)

- If the meaning is *to know how to*, use **savoir** (→ 12)

- *Can* + a 'verb of hearing or seeing etc.' in English is not translated in French (→ 13)

1 **Il est tard**   **C'est peu probable**
It's late   It's not very likely

2 **Où se trouve la gare?**
Where's the station?

3 **Quel temps fait-il?**   **Il fait beau/mauvais/du vent**
What's the weather like?   It's lovely/miserable/windy

4 **Quel âge avez-vous?**   **J'ai quinze ans**
How old are you?   I'm fifteen

5 **Comment allez-vous?**   **Je vais très bien**
How are you?   I'm very well

6 **Où est mon parapluie? – Il est là, dans le coin**
Where's my umbrella? – It's there, in the corner
Descends la valise si elle n'est pas trop lourde
Bring down the case if it isn't too heavy

7 **Quelle heure est-il? – Il est sept heures et demie**
What's the time? – It's half past seven

8 **Il est difficile de répondre à cette question**
It's difficult to reply to this question

9 **C'est moi qui ne l'aime pas**
It's me who doesn't like him
C'est Charles/ma mère qui l'a dit
It's Charles/my mother who said so
C'est ici que je les ai achetés
It's here that I bought them
C'est parce que la poste est fermée que ...
It's because the post office is closed that ...

10 **Il y a quelqu'un à la porte**
There's somebody at the door
Il y a cinq livres sur la table
There are five books on the table

11 **Pouvez-vous atteindre cette étagère?**
Can you reach up to that shelf?

12 **Elle ne sait pas nager**
She can't swim

13 **Je ne vois rien**   **Il les entendait**
I can't see anything   He could hear them

to (see also below)

- Generally translated by **à** (→ **1**)
  (See p. 204)

- In time expressions, e.g. *10 to 6*, use **moins** (→ **2**)

- When the meaning is *in order to*, use **pour** (→ **3**)

- Following a verb, as in *to try to do, to like to do*, see pp. 44 and 64

- *easy/difficult/impossible* etc. *to do*:
  The preposition used depends on whether a specific noun is
  referred to (→ **4**) or not (→ **5**)

at/in/to

- With feminine countries, use **en** (→ **6**)
  With masculine countries, use **au** (**aux** with plural countries) (→ **7**)

- With towns, use **à** (→ **8**)

- *at/to the butcher's/grocer's* etc.: use **à** + noun designating the
  shop, or **chez** + noun designating the shopkeeper (→ **9**)

- *at/to the dentist's/doctor's* etc.: use **chez** (→ **10**)

- *at/to ...'s/...s' house*: use **chez** (→ **11**)

1 **Donne le livre à Patrick**
Give the book to Patrick

2 **dix heures moins cinq**   **à sept heures moins le quart**
five to ten   at a quarter to seven

3 **Je l'ai fait pour vous aider**
I did it to help you
Il se pencha pour nouer son lacet
He bent down to tie his shoelace

4 **Ce livre est difficile à lire**
This book is difficult to read

5 **Il est difficile de comprendre leurs raisons**
It's difficult to understand their reasons

6 **Il est allé en France/en Suisse**
He has gone to France/to Switzerland
un village en Norvège/en Belgique
a village in Norway/in Belgium

7 **Etes-vous allé au Canada/au Danemark/aux Etats-Unis?**
Have you been to Canada/to Denmark/to the United States?
une ville au Japon/au Brésil
a town in Japan/in Brazil

8 **Il est allé à Vienne/à Bruxelles**
He has gone to Vienna/to Brussels
Il habite à Londres/à Genève
He lives in London/in Geneva
Ils logent dans un hôtel à St. Pierre
They're staying in a hotel at St. Pierre

9 **Je l'ai acheté** { **à l'épicerie** / **chez l'épicier** }   I bought it at the grocer's
Elle est allée { **à la boulangerie** / **chez le boulanger** }   She's gone to the baker's

10 **J'ai un rendez-vous chez le dentiste**
I've an appointment at the dentist's
Il est allé chez le médecin
He has gone to the doctor's

11 **chez Christian**   **chez les Pagot**
at/to Christian's house   at/to the Pagots' house

General Points

● Activity of the lips

The lips play a very important part in French. When a vowel is described as having 'rounded' lips, the lips are slightly drawn together and pursed, as when an English speaker expresses exaggerated surprise with the vowel 'ooh!'. Equally, if the lips are said to be 'spread', the corners are pulled firmly back towards the cheeks, tendng to reveal the front teeth.

In English, lip position is not important, and vowel sounds tend to merge because of this. In French, the activity of the lips means that every vowel sound is clearly distinct from every other.

● No diphthongs

A diphthong is a glide between two vowel sounds in the same syllable. In English, there are few 'pure' vowel sounds, but largely diphthongs instead. Although speakers of English may *think* they produce one vowel sound in the word 'day', in fact they use a diphthong, which in this instance is a glide between the vowels [e] and [ɪ]: [deɪ]. In French the tension maintained in the lips, tongue and the mouth in general prevents diphthongs occurring, as the vowel sound is kept constant throughout. Hence the French word corresponding to the above example, 'dé', is pronounced with no final [ɪ] sound, but is phonetically represented thus: [de].

● Consonants

In English, consonants are often pronounced with a degree of laxness that can result in their practically disappearing altogether although not strictly 'silent'. In a relaxed pronunciation of a word such as 'hat', the 't' is often scarcely heard, or is replaced by a 'glottal stop' (a sort of jerk in the throat). This never occurs in French, where consonants are always given their full value.

Pronunciation of Consonants

Some consonants are pronounced almost exactly as in English: [b, p, f, v, g, k, m, w].
Most others are similar to English, but slight differences should be noted.

EXAMPLES	HINTS ON PRONUNCIATION
[d] **d**in**d**e	
[t] **t**en**t**e	The tip of the tongue touches the upper front teeth and not the roof of the mouth as in English
[n] **n**o**nn**e	
[l] **L**i**ll**e	
[s] tou**s** **ç**a	The tip of the tongue is down behind the bottom front teeth, lower than in English
[z] **z**éro ro**s**e	
[ʃ] **ch**ose ta**ch**e	Like the *sh* of English *shout*
[ʒ] **j**e **g**ilet bei**g**e	Like the *s* of English *measure*
[j] **y**eux pai**ll**e	Like the *y* of English *yes*

Three consonants are not heard in English:

[ʀ] **r**a**r**e veni**r**	*R* is often silent in English, e.g. fa*r*m. In French the [ʀ] is never silent, unless it follows an **e** at the end of a word e.g. cherch**er**. To pronounce it, try to make a short sound like gargling. Similar, too, to the Scottish pronunciation of lo**ch**
[ɲ] vi**gn**e a**gn**eau	Similar to the *ni* of Span*i*ard
[ɥ] h**u**ile l**u**eur	Like a very rapid [y] (see p. 239) followed immediately by the next vowel of the word

Pronunciation of Vowels

EXAMPLES	HINTS ON PRONUNCIATION
[a] **pa**tte pl**a**t **a**mour	Similar to the vowel in English *pat*
[ɑ] b**a**s p**â**te	Longer than the sound above, it resembles the English exclamation of surprise *ah!* Similar, too, to the English vowel in *car* without the final *r* sound
[ɛ] l**ai**t jou**e**t m**e**rci	Similar to the English vowel in *pet*. Beware of using the English diphthong [eɪ] as in *pay*
[e] **é**t**é** jou**e**r	A pure vowel, again quite different from the diphthong in English *pay*
[ə] l**e** pr**e**mier	Similar to the English sound in butt*er* when the *r* is not pronounced
[i] **i**c**i** v**i**e lyc**é**e	The lips are well spread towards the cheeks while uttering this sound. Shorter than the English vowel in *see*
[ɔ] m**o**rt h**o**mme	The lips are well rounded while producing a sound similar to the *o* of English *cot*
[o] m**o**t d**ô**me **eau**	A pure vowel with strongly rounded lips; quite different from the diphthong in English *bone, low*

[u] gen**ou** r**ou**e	A pure vowel with strongly rounded lips. Similar to the English *ooh!* of surprise
[y] r**u**e vêt**u**	Often the most difficult for English speakers to produce: round your lips and try to pronounce [i] (see above). There is no [j] sound (see p. 237) as there is in English *pure*
[œ] s**œu**r b**eu**rre	Similar to the vowel in English *fir* or *murmur*, but without the *r* sound and with the lips more strongly rounded
[ø] p**eu** d**eu**x	To pronounce this, try to say [e] (see above) with the lips strongly rounded

Nasal Vowels

These are spelt with a vowel followed by a 'nasal' consonant – **n** or **m**. The production of nasal vowels really requires the help of a teacher or a recording of the sound. However, to help you, the vowel is pronounced by allowing the air from the lungs to come partly down the nose and partly through the mouth, and the **n** or **m** is not pronounced at all.

[ɑ̃] l**en**t s**an**g d**an**s	
[ɛ̃] mat**in** pl**ein**	In each case, the vowel shown in the phonetic symbol is pronounced as described above, but air is allowed to come through the nose as well as the mouth
[ɔ̃] n**on** p**on**t	
[œ̃] br**un** **un** parf**um**	

From Spelling to Sounds

Although it may not seem so at first sight, there are some fairly precise 'rules' which can help you to know how to pronounce French words from their spelling.

Vowels

SPELLING	PRONOUNCED	EXAMPLES
a, à	[a]	chatte, table
a, â	[ɑ]	pâte, pas
e, é	[e]	été, marcher
e, é, ê	[ɛ]	fenêtre, fermer, chère
e	[ɔ]	double, fenêtre
i, î, y	[i]	lit. abîmer, lycée
o, ô	[o]	pot, trop, dôme
o	[ɔ]	sotte, orange
u, û	[y]	battu, fût, pur

Vowel Groups

There are several groups of vowels in French spelling which are regularly pronounced in the same way:

ai	[ɛ] or [e]	maison, marchai, faire
ail	[aj]	portail
ain, aim, (c)in, im	[ɛ̃]	pain, faim, frein, impair
au	[o]	auberge, landau
an, am, en, em	[ɑ̃]	plan, ample, entrer, temps
eau	[o]	bateau, eau
eu	[œ] or [ø]	feu, peur
euil(le), ueil	[œj]	feuille, recueil
oi, oy	[wa]	voire, voyage
on, om	[ɔ̃]	ton, compter
ou	[u]	hibou, outil
œu	[œ]	sœur, cœur
ue	[y]	rue
un, um	[œ̃]	brun, parfum

Added to these are the many groups of letters occurring at the end of words, where their pronunciation is predictable, bearing in mind the tendency (see p. 242) of final consonants to remain silent:

TYPICAL WORDS	PRONUNCIATION OF FINAL SYLLABLE
pas, mât, chat	[ɑ] or [a]
marcher, marchez marchais, marchait, baie, valet, mes, fumée	[e] or [ɛ]
nid	[i]
chaud, vaut, faux, sot, tôt, Pernod, dos, croc	[o]
bout, bijoux, sous, boue	[u]
fut, fût, crus, crûs	[y]
queue, heureux, bleus	[ø]
en, vend, vent, an, sang, grand, dans	[ɑ̃]
fin, feint, frein, vain	[ɛ̃]
on, pont, fond, avons	[ɔ̃]
brun, parfum	[œ̃]

Continued

From Spelling to Sounds (ctd.)

Consonants

● Final consonants are usually silent (→1)

● **n** or **m** at the end of a syllable or word are silent, but they have the effect of 'nasalizing' the preceding vowel(s) (see p. 239 on Nasal Vowels)

● The letter **h** is either 'silent' ('mute') or 'aspirate' when it begins a word. When silent, the word behaves as though it started with a vowel and takes a liaison with the preceding word where appropriate.
When the **h** is aspirate, no liaison is made (→2)
There is no way of predicting which words start with which sort of **h** – this simply has to be learnt with each word

● The following consonants in spelling have predictable pronunciations: b, d, f, k, l, p, r, t, v, w, x, y, z. Others vary:

SPELLING	PRONOUNCED	ENGLISH EXAMPLES	
c + a, o, u	[k]	can, cot, cut	
+ l, r		class, cram	(→3)
c + e, i, y	[s]	ceiling, ice	(→4)
ç + a, o, u	[s]	ceiling, ice	(→5)
ch	[ʃ]	shop, lash	(→6)
g + a, o, u	[g]	gate, got, gun	
+ l, r		glass, gramme	(→7)
g + e, i, y	[ʒ]	leisure	(→8)
gn	[n]	companion, onion	(→9)
j	[ʒ]	measure	(→10)
q, qu	[k]	quay, kit	(→11)
s between vowels:	[z]	rose	
elsewhere	[s]	sit	(→12)
th	[t]	Thomas	(→13)
t in -tion	[s]	sit	(→14)

1 éclat
[ekla]
chaud
[ʃo]
2 silent **h**:
des hôtels
[de zotɛl]

nez
[ne]
aider
[ɛde]
aspirate **h**:
des haricots
[de aʀiko]

3 café
[kafe]
classe
[klas]

côte
[kot]
croûte
[kʀut]

culture
[kyltyʀ]

4 ceci
[səsi]

cil
[sil]

cycliste
[siklist]

5 ça
[sa]

garçon
[gaʀsɔ̃]

déçu
[desy]

6 chat
[ʃa]

riche
[ʀiʃ]

7 gare
[gaʀ]
glaise
[glɛz]

gourde
[guʀd]
gramme
[gʀam]

aigu
[ɛgy]

8 gemme
[ʒɛm]

gilet
[ʒilɛ]

gymnaste
[ʒimnast]

9 vigne
[viɲ]

oignon
[ɔɲɔ̃]

10 joli
[ʒɔli]

Jules
[ʒyl]

11 quiche
[kiʃ]

quitter
[kite]

12 sable
[sablə]

maison
[mɛzɔ̃]

13 théâtre
[teɑtʀ]

Thomas
[tɔma]

14 nation
[nasjɔ̃]

action
[aksjɔ̃]

Feminine Forms and Pronunciation

● For adjectives and nouns ending in a vowel in the masculine, the addition of an **e** to form the feminine does not alter the pronunciation (→**1**)

● If the masculine ends with a silent consonant, generally **-d**, **-s**, **-r** or **-t**, the consonant is sounded in the feminine (→**2**)
This also applies when the final consonant is doubled before the addition of the feminine **e** (→**3**)

● If the masculine ends in a nasal vowel and a silent **n**, e.g. **-an**, **-on**, **-in**, the vowel is no longer nasalized and the **-n** is pronounced in the feminine (→**4**)
This also applies when the final **-n** is doubled before the addition of the feminine **e** (→**5**)

● Where the masculine and feminine forms have totally different endings (see pp. 136 and 150), the pronunciation of course varies accordingly (→**6**)

Plural Forms and Pronunciation

● The addition of **s** or **x** to form regular plurals generally does not affect pronunciation (→**7**)

● Where liaison has to be made, the final **-s** or **-x** of the plural form is pronounced (→**8**)

● Where the masculine singular and plural forms have totally different endings (see pp. 138 and 148), the pronunciation of course varies accordingly (→**9**)

● Note the change in pronunciation in the following nouns:

SINGULAR		PLURAL		
bœuf	[bœf]	**bœufs**	[bø]	ox/oxen
œuf	[œf]	**œufs**	[ø]	egg/eggs
os	[ɔs]	**os**	[o]	bone/bones

ADJECTIVES		NOUNS	
1 joli	→ **jolie**	**un ami**	→ **une amie**
[ʒɔli]	[ʒɔli]	[ami]	[ami]
déçu	→ **déçue**	**un employé**	→ **une employée**
[desy]	[desy]	[ãplwaje]	[ãplwaje]
2 chaud	→ **chaude**	**un étudiant**	→ **une étudiante**
[ʃo]	[ʃod]	[etydjã]	[etydjãt]
français	→ **française**	**un Anglais**	→ **une Anglaise**
[frãsɛ]	[frãsɛz]	[ãglɛ]	[ãglɛz]
inquiet	→ **inquiète**	**un étranger**	→ **une étrangère**
[ɛ̃kjɛ]	[ɛ̃kjɛt]	[etrãʒe]	[etrãʒɛʀ]
3 violet	→ **violette**	**le cadet**	→ **la cadette**
[vjɔlɛ]	[vjɔlɛt]	[kadɛ]	[kadɛt]
gras	→ **grasse**		→
[grɑ]	[grɑs]		
4 plein	→ **pleine**	**le souverain**	→ **la souveraine**
[plɛ̃]	[plɛn]	[suvrɛ̃]	[suvrɛn]
fin	→ **fine**	**Le Persan**	→ **la Persane**
[fɛ̃]	[fin]	[pɛrsã]	[pɛrsan]
brun	→ **brune**	**le voisin**	→ **la voisine**
[brœ̃]	[bryn]	[vwazɛ̃]	[vwazin]
5 canadien	→ **canadienne**	**le paysan**	→ **la paysanne**
[kanadjɛ̃]	[kanadjɛn]	[peizã]	[peizan]
breton	→ **bretonne**	**le baron**	→ **la baronne**
[brətɔ̃]	[brətɔn]	[barɔ̃]	[barɔn]
6 vif	→ **vive**	**le veuf**	→ **la veuve**
[vif]	[viv]	[vœf]	[vœv]
traître	→ **traîtresse**	**le maître**	→ **la maîtresse**
[trɛtrə]	[trɛtrɛs]	[mɛtrə]	[mɛtrɛs]
7 beau	→ **beaux**	**la maison**	→ **les maisons**
[bo]	[bo]	[mɛzɔ̃]	[mɛzɔ̃]
8 des anciens élèves			
[de zãsjɛ̃ zelɛv]			
de beaux arbres			
[də bo zarbʀ(ə)]			
9 amical	→ **amicaux**	**un journal**	→ **des journaux**
[amikal]	[amiko]	[ʒurnal]	[ʒurno]

The Alphabet

A, a	[ɑ]	**J, j**	[ʒi]	**S, s**	[ɛs]
B, b	[be]	**K, k**	[ka]	**T, t**	[te]
C, c	[se]	**L, l**	[ɛl]	**U, u**	[y]
D, d	[de]	**M, m**	[ɛm]	**V, v**	[ve]
E, e	[ə]	**N, n**	[ɛn]	**W, w**	[dubləve]
F, f	[ɛf]	**O, o**	[o]	**X, x**	[iks]
G, g	[ʒe]	**P, p**	[pe]	**Y, y**	[igrɛk]
H, h	[aʃ]	**Q, q**	[ky]	**Z, z**	[zɛd]
I, i	[i]	**R, r**	[ɛr]		

Capital letters are used as in English *except* for the following:

● adjectives of nationality
  e.g. **une ville espagnole**   **un auteur français**
       a Spanish town   a French author

● languages
  e.g. **Parlez-vous anglais?**   **Il parle français et allemand**
       Do you speak English?   He speaks French and German

● days of the week:

lundi	Monday
mardi	Tuesday
mercredi	Wednesday
jeudi	Thursday
vendredi	Friday
samedi	Saturday
dimanche	Sunday

● months of the year:

janvier	January	**juillet**	July
février	February	**août**	August
mars	March	**septembre**	September
avril	April	**octobre**	October
mai	May	**novembre**	November
juin	June	**décembre**	December

The following index lists comprehensively both grammatical terms and key words in French and English contained in this book.